D0984253

A PENNY FOR A SONG

THE HEREFORD PLAYS

General Editor: E. R. Wood

THUNDER ROCK

Robert Ardrey

A MAN FOR ALL SEASONS

THE TIGER AND THE HORSE

Robert Bolt

HOBSON'S CHOICE

Harold Brighouse

BILLY BUDD

Robert Chapman *and* Louis Coxe

DICKON

Gordon Daviot

THE LONG AND THE SHORT AND THE TALL

Willis Hall

TIME AND THE CONWAYS

AN INSPECTOR CALLS

J. B. Priestley

NEXT TIME I'LL SING TO YOU

A SCENT OF FLOWERS

James Saunders

JOURNEY'S END

R. C. Sherriff

RIDERS TO THE SEA *and*

THE PLAYBOY OF THE WESTERN WORLD

J. M. Synge

ROMANOFF AND JULIET

Peter Ustinov

MARCHING SONG

SAINT'S DAY

A PENNY FOR A SONG

John Whiting

THREE DRAMATIC LEGENDS

Sacrifice to the Wind – André Obey

Scandal at Coventry – Clemence Dane

The Countess Cathleen – W. B. Yeats

JOHN WHITING

A Penny for a Song

A COMEDY

WITH AN INTRODUCTION AND NOTES BY

E. R. WOOD

HEINEMANN EDUCATIONAL
BOOKS LTD · LONDON

Heinemann Educational Books Ltd
LONDON MELBOURNE TORONTO
SINGAPORE CAPE TOWN
AUCKLAND IBADAN
HONG KONG

A Penny for a Song first published
in *The Plays of John Whiting* (Heinemann) 1957

This new version first published in
The Hereford Plays 1964
Reprinted 1966 (twice)

110483

Published by
Heinemann Educational Books Ltd
48 Charles Street, London W.1
Printed in Great Britain by
Bookprint Limited, Crawley, Sussex

INTRODUCTION

THE DEATH of John Whiting in June 1963 was a tragic loss to the English theatre, which had belatedly come to appreciate him after years of neglect. His early dramas came before theatre-goers and critics were ready for them: *Saint's Day*, though it won the Arts Theatre's Festival of Britain Prize in 1951, was brutally battered by the critics, and ran for only three weeks; *Marching Song* in 1954 was treated with more respect, but fell short of commercial success. Today the public would not be daunted by the obscurity and austerity for which these plays were originally attacked. The comedies were no more fortunate. When *A Penny for a Song* was presented at the Haymarket in 1951 it unaccountably failed to run for more than a month; *The Gates of Summer* (1956) did not reach London: it closed during a preliminary provincial tour when Dorothy Tutin, playing a leading role, became too ill to go on. John Whiting, dogged by bad luck and the incomprehension of the majority, turned to films as a means of earning his living. He had achieved great prestige among a few, mainly actors and theatre directors, but not with the general public or the business men who run theatres.

John Whiting's career illustrates the disadvantages of the commercial theatre, in which luck is an important element and where there is not much chance for a writer who does not either catch the fashion of the times or adapt himself to time-honoured recipes for success. In this strange world a completely undistinguished thriller or farce may run for ten years for no discoverable reason, or a new play of genuine quality may unexpectedly catch the public fancy and draw the fashionable crowds; but there can be no kind of assurance that important plays by new or even major dramatists will be presented at all, or that if presented they will be given a chance to establish themselves, or will ever be revived after a first run, even if it is a successful run. Add to these hazards the damage that may be done by critics, who may damn a play because they do not understand or appreciate its first performance, and it may seem surprising that new writers get a hearing at all.

Fortunately there are theatres in London and the provinces where commercial considerations are less insistent and where a play may be allowed to find its feet after some initial stumbling. In 1961 the Royal Shakespeare Company commissioned John Whiting to write a new play for production at the Aldwych Theatre, and the result was *The Devils*, his first popular success. In 1962 the same theatre revived *A Penny for a Song*. The text was revised and extensively altered, especially in the parts concerning Edward Sterne, and it is the new version that is printed here.

At the time of his death, John Whiting was at work on another play for the Aldwych, and had been commissioned to translate a Molière comedy for their repertory; he had just completed a film script on the life of Sean O'Casey, and he was apparently well established as a major dramatist with a fruitful career ahead of him.

He died of cancer at the age of 45.

Characters and Themes

In the author's introduction to *The Plays of John Whiting* (Heinemann, 1957) he says of the original version of *A Penny for a Song*: 'It was written at a time of great personal happiness, and by then it seemed natural that such a feeling should be expressed in a play. I was entirely uncritical of life as I was living it then, and the whole world seemed to be in love. War appeared the greatest absurdity.' In this mood he evidently took delight in laughing at human folly (though at other times he found it tragic), and the atmosphere of the play is one of fun and charm. Nevertheless, John Whiting was accustomed to warn people of 'the common error of believing that laughter is kind', and when he revised the play in 1962 he did not intend it to be enjoyed merely as a charming romance. In the hilarious comedy, sometimes verging on farce, there is a satirical sting, and the play contains some intellectual discussion of serious themes.

The people in the play fall into two distinct groups: the eccentrics and the representatives of good sense. The characteristic of the eccentrics is that each is obsessed with an interest which he pursues beyond all reason and without being deflected by other claims on his attention; these people are like hounds, so intent upon following a scent that they cannot look up, or like children preoccupied with some absorbing game. Thus for Sir Timothy Bellboys only one thing matters, his scheme for fighting the French single-handed; for his brother the prospect of invasion means more scope for fire-fighting; while Hester's mind is taken up with the need to join Lady Jerningham's Amazon Corps in East Anglia.

Sir Timothy is all the funnier for being so deadly serious about his crazy scheme, so indignant about being superseded in command of his Bellboys Fencibles, so contemptuous of his brother for wanting to fight fires instead of Frenchmen. When he thinks that someone else is masquerading as Napoleon he says it is 'damned impertinence'; when Humpage shows him the wind-direction he objects: 'According to my calculations the wind cannot be blowing from that direction today.' He assumes that only he matters and only he is right. He is a caricature of the English country gentleman in his maltreatment of the French language, in his pride in the public school he attended as a boy, and in his eagerness to forget all else at the end in order to talk about cricket. In real life he would be insufferable, but as a stage character he is attractive because he has such vigour, such gusto, such physical courage, all a little larger than life. John Whiting said: 'I have written of other heroic figures, but none please me more than Sir Timothy Bellboys.'

His brother Lamprett is in fact a more engaging person, because he is milder and less arrogant – a kind of gentle Don Quixote – but he is just as single-minded as Sir Timothy. When a loud explosion is followed by the arrival of a couple of cannon balls he gets up and shuts the garden gate without being deflected from what he is saying about his fire brigade; and when Selincourt protests to him, 'You are the man who has been putting out all my fires', he overwhelms him with the reply, 'Your fires, sir? The law holds that a fire, once under way, is public property.'

An extra dimension is given to the comic eccentricity of the two brothers by the impatience of each with the other's obsession. Each regards Humpage as his own look-out, the one demanding reports of ships or troops, the other of fires. When Sir Timothy tells Humpage to ring the alarum bell, Lamprett protests: 'No, Humpage. No. You'll call out the brigade. Damn the invasion!' The ensuing quarrel ends in Sir Timothy calling his brother 'a damned ignorant fool' and adding, 'Anyway, I've no time for a row with you,' to which Lamprett answers like a sulky child, 'Well, don't say horrid things about my brigade, then.'

The spectacle of grown men squabbling like schoolboys is comic on the stage. Their behaviour is of the essence of the Comic, as described in Henri Bergson's classic study, *Le Rire*, in which he says: 'Any individual is comic who automatically goes his own way without troubling himself about getting into touch with his fellow-beings.' Such automatism and preoccupation with one's own interests would be less funny in actual life, especially if the national crisis were real and immediate. The absurdity of war preparations is not so outrageously exaggerated here as might be supposed. Inter-service rivalries can be almost as ludicrous as those between Sir

Timothy, Lamprett and Selincourt; and military plans can be almost as inadequate as theirs. The play contains satirical shafts at other aspects of war, such as the jargon ('the situation is fluid'), the military reports as burlesqued in Brotherhood's account of his encounter with the French Emperor, the preoccupation with details of uniform, especially in women's forces, and the methods of testing a supposed spy to see if he is English. The local defence volunteers under Selincourt are grotesquely comic, but they inspire no less confidence than some of the well-meaning organizations of today with their plans to deal with the results of nuclear attack. By placing the events and characters in a setting of long ago the author softens the blows of his satire.

Much of the play deals, then, with the absurdity of war in a light, even hilarious vein; but set against the eccentrics we have two characters who know what war is really like – Edward Sterne and the little boy. Dorcas has no experience of fighting or poverty, but she is intuitive enough to see the difference between those who play at hostilities and those who have suffered the real thing. 'That boy', she says, 'has stood on battlefields, he's walked continents, he's been threatened and survived, he's seen the dead, he's swum rivers and gone hungry. My God, he makes you look innocent. He makes you look – like children.' This is where the laughter is sharply pulled up. The strange paradox is that the young understand reality: it is the old who treat life and death as a child's game. We are reminded that the dangers involved in playing at hostilities form one of the themes of *Saint's Day*.

John Whiting was also deeply concerned with the problem of responsibility for war and suffering. In *A Penny for a Song* he seems to be expressing some of his experience of the war of 1939–45 through Edward Sterne, who says:

For the last four years I've been walking about Europe. I've seen such horrible things that it broke my heart. Poverty and disease, love and friendship ruined by war, men and women living like animals in a desperate attempt to stay alive. I was one who sold himself for war so that he could eat, and I've had women sell themselves to me so that their children could eat. Now I may be simple, Matthews, but there's cause for all this. And the cause is laziness and indifference. There are only a handful of tyrants at any one time, but there are millions who don't care.

Is the play to be taken, then, as an appeal for the kind of humanitarian radicalism that Edward Sterne has learnt from reading Tom Paine? Clearly Edward's experience, good sense and concern for others provide a standard against which the follies of the eccentrics are shown up and the cultured escapism of Hallam Matthews is reproved. It is not surprising that Dorcas says: 'I think you are a most wonderful man.' He has saved a little boy's life, but he discounts any claim to virtue. 'I just found him, that's all,' he explains. His advice about how to behave in the midst of fighting is practical and free of heroics, not unlike that of Bluntschli in Shaw's *Arms and the Man*. He says:

> Don't stand under a flag, stay far away from anybody in a fine bright uniform, take a look at the sun so that you'll always know which way you're running, if there's a loaf of bread about put it in your pocket, and if there's a hole in the ground sit in it. Ignore all cries for help, stay deaf to all exhortations, and keep your trousers tied tight about your waist. In any difficulty, look stupid, and at the first opportunity go to sleep.

This is the kind of paradox that is packed with common sense. It is, as Edward says, 'the philosophy of a common soldier'. Men are more likely to conquer the world with it than with the inflated heroics of Sir Timothy and Selincourt.

Edward thinks that the problem of war and poverty can be solved by spreading the ideas of Tom Paine, based on reason and a belief in mankind. When he quotes an eloquent passage from *The Rights of Man* Dorcas exclaims: 'That's beautiful. It's like poetry.'

It was an inspiring book, and in the early nineteenth century a revolutionary one; but although Edward Sterne is an attractive character whose arguments appear persuasive, it would be a mistake to suppose that he is meant to 'know all the answers'. John Whiting does not offer to his audience clear-cut solutions to the problems posed. He distrusted clear-cut solutions, and he suffered, he said, from being able to see both sides of a question. So we are not to swallow all that Edward says. Even Dorcas cautions him: 'Don't become one of those men for whom the idea of people gets to be more important than people themselves.' This is a danger that besets friends of humanity, and that made Whiting draw back from humanitarian movements.

Hence there arises the debate with Hallam Matthews. He is another man of sense, beside whom the eccentrics appear all the more absurd. His calm irony makes him a theatrically effective foil in scenes with Sir Timothy, Lamprett and Selincourt. But he is also set in contrast to Edward and Dorcas. He stands for the conservatism and scepticism of middle age against the young people with 'their passion for causes, most of them lost'. He has read Tom Paine, Jeremy Bentham and Rousseau; he still makes a point of keeping up with Wordsworth (once a revolutionary); so his disagreement with the reformers is not based on ignorance. He does not believe you can improve the world by conviction, because if you start with the people they are slow to follow; if you start at the top you are confronted with a head of state who is a 'dear, silly man'; if you reject the hereditary principle (as represented by George III) you find democracy turning up 'this frightful little Bonaparte person'. Hallam values tradition and likes the world very much as it is.

This subtle, civilized Tory solves no problems either. He is running away from reality. 'Like most men of my age I am in flight, pursued by the agony of love, the danger of war and the misery of democracy.' He admits to Dorcas that if he had

stayed as vulnerable as he was when he was young he would
not have survived. So he has adopted as a sort of defensive
shell a habit of ironical joking to avoid facing serious matters.
Thus he says of democracy, 'We all believe in it, my dear,
but some of us are too well-mannered to practise it'; of his
money, 'It doesn't come from the sweat of the poor. I get it
by gambling, and loans from friends. It's all perfectly respectable;' and of his reasons for leaving the army, 'Actually, it was
the food. I found it too disgusting for words.' He is anxious
that nothing shall deter him 'from fully enjoying this charming occupation called life'. So he tries to ignore poverty and
war and he says, 'I live my own life. I don't try to live other
people's lives for them.' Evidently not one of those to whom
(in Keats's phrase) 'the miseries of the world are misery, and
will not let them rest.' All the same, he seems to envy the
young their capacity for love and their enthusiasm for causes.

One recognizes something of the author himself in both
Edward Sterne and Hallam Matthews. John Whiting in his
youth went through a period of enthusiasm for left-wing
politics, but in his forties he was closer to the disillusionment
and scepticism of Matthews. The middle-aged conservatism is
a corrective to the reforming zeal of the young man; but it is
more sterile and backward-looking; the young people have
more vitality and appeal. Dorcas sums up Hallam's pose
of being only concerned with himself, when she exclaims:

> Now wars can break out, monsters can land in the country, the
> marvels of science and art can threaten us all with destruction, but
> none of it matters so long as Hallam Matthews gets through
> luncheon without indigestion.

He answers as usual with a joke: 'You've obviously never had
indigestion.'

The value of this character in terms of the stage is obviously
high; in terms of the debate on war and peace, tradition and

revolution, private comfort or general progress, youthful ardour or middle-aged caution, the balance seems to tip on the side of the young ones.

Since Dorcas, the most charming character in the play, falls in love with Edward, the unwary playgoer may expect a sweetly romantic ending. But John Whiting makes no concessions to the sentimental. Edward does not (at any rate in the 1962 version) fall in love with Dorcas, and does not pretend that he does. Dorcas is sensible enough to face this fact. She can see both the realities and the falsities of love. 'After all', she says, 'I'm still young enough to talk about a very common experience as if it were the most original thing in the world.' The honest relationship between the two is more moving than a conventional romance and it provides that rare theatrical experience, a love scene without illusions. Dorcas's awakening and 'putting off childish ways' is all the more poignant.

The little boy is a remarkably appealing figure on the stage, not because he is given any pretty childish words to say or things to do, but because he brings out all that is kind and gentle in others. Even when Lamprett pulls his leg about wine-drinking, the stage direction says: '*They laugh gently at the child*'. Everybody talks to him as if he were an adult and understood English. It makes no difference to anybody that he is 'a little enemy'. Here at least they recognize that humanity is all one. The author has succeeded in creating a moving and attractive figure of childhood without the sentimentality which is common in the treatment of children in theatre and cinema, and from which the original version of the play was not entirely free.

Style

The dialogue is a representation of the real language of men, but it is, of course, more graceful than the reality. Most of the characters use an educated English of no particular period or region. Even a servant will say, 'Does the emergency warrant so grave a liberty?' The wit of the lines often depends on irony or on paradox, as when Lamprett speaks of 'ephemeral activities such as agriculture' or Hallam warns Edward of the danger of filling Dorcas with 'ideas which are below her station'. Within the general style, each character has characteristics of speech which are expressive of the individual. Hallam, for instance, talks in a consciously literary manner, ironical, with a touch of self-mockery, as when he speaks to the little boy:

> I can't make you laugh, but de la Rochefoucauld can. And there's all this talk about the equality of man. That worries me very much. What ground do you and I meet on? It's a problem, isn't it? Forty years must separate us. We know nothing about each other, and seem quite incapable of telling. Those eyes of yours have seen more than they should. I don't know why I feel that, but somehow I understand why you reject the weather, the war and other trivial matters, such as love and justice, as subjects for conversation.

Lamprett calls himself 'a man of learning turned man of action by necessity', and this amusing conception of himself is reflected in his way of speaking. Sir Timothy's language is full of his energy and ebullience, with a habit of dramatizing himself:

> Tell the family that I am well – desperately tired but well and, as yet, unharmed. I have made contact with the enemy troops twice, and a more slovenly, cowardly, uncouth crew I never did see. I don't know why there's been all this fuss about encountering Bonaparte's much-vaunted army.

Selincourt is not unlike him in class and temperament, and his style is similar. Hester is given to oracular pronouncements, euphoniously phrased and decorated with paradox, which belong to the tradition of elegant comedy from Wycherley to Wilde; for instance:

There is great comfort, I find, in resorting to good food during a crisis. Man's behaviour to man would be less ungenerous if everyone ate regular meals. For when conversation fails, how much better to resort to the knife and fork than to the sword and trumpet.

This kind of talk, both in matter and in manner, is sharply contrasted with that of Edward Sterne, who is different in experience, class and age. His outlook is like that of an ex-soldier of our own times, but this is not expressed in the colloquial barrack-room language so familiar in many recent plays, but rather in plain but educated speech. In his first conversation with Dorcas he is noticeably dry and laconic, and when he argues with Hallam his bluntness is set against the mannered, polished sentences of the older and consciously-cultured gentleman. The difference is partly one of generation too; for the young Dorcas talks in unsophisticated language more like Edward's than that of her own family. The young express themselves in a style that seems more direct and more sincere, just as they seem more genuine as persons. It is a remarkable achievement to have contrived a general style which can include such different elements and yet remain harmonious, which can please the ear with its grace and wit, and yet carry a real argument with sincerity and force.

Theatrical Qualities

The play is constructed with great technical sureness. The basic theatrical situation of Sir Timothy disguised as Napoleon meeting forces that he believes to be invading Frenchmen, while George Selincourt's intended exercise becomes the Real Thing when his men stumble on what appears to be the French Emperor himself, is built up to a magnificent comic climax when George Selincourt confronts Sir Timothy. The tests by which Sir Timothy proves that he is an Englishman provide a most effective scene in the theatre. The essential plot is embellished by the interwoven situation of Lamprett putting out fires as fast as Selincourt can light them. The

comedy of situation, character and dialogue is enlivened by
stage business, such as Lamprett's firework for blowing up
fires, designed to have the sound added later, the elaborate
fire-engine working in the garden amid preparations for an
alfresco meal, and Sir Timothy's sudden descent of the well,
followed by a loud explosion which brings the first act to a
comically sensational conclusion. Sir Timothy's reappearance
in the gondola of a balloon and his involuntary descent of the
well a second time is all the funnier for the calm of the other
characters: Hester says, 'Oh, so you're back', and as he disappears again Selincourt comes in protesting, 'Some fool is
going round putting out all my signal fires.' Much of the
business associated with Humpage is of the essence of stage
clowning, and Hester's solemn instruction to shut the gate to
keep out the cannon balls belongs to surrealist farce.

But the tone of the play is well varied and the serious
passages have their own atmosphere, at some moments like
Shaw, at others like Chekhov.

The bright summer morning of the opening, and the falling
dark of the end, with candlelight in the windows and music
from the house, offer splendid scope for the resources of
lighting and stage setting. The Aldwych production of 1962
was a memorable theatrical experience, with all the sparkling
fun and stimulating argument closing in unspoken poetry.

Hey, nonny no!
Men are fools that wish to die!
Is't not fine to dance and sing
When the bells of death do ring?

ANONYMOUS

For oure tyme is a very shadow that passeth away,
and after our ende there is no returnynge, for it
is fast sealed, so that no man commeth agayne.
Come on therefore, let us enjoye the pleasures
that there are, and let us soone use the creature
like as in youth. . . . Let us leave some token of
oure pleasure in every place, for that is oure
porcion, els gett we nothinge.

THE BOKE OF WYSDOME

All things can tempt me from this craft of verse:
One time it was a woman's face, or worse –
The seeming needs of my fool-driven land;
Now nothing but comes readier to the hand
Than this accustomed toil. When I was young,
I had not given a penny for a song
Did not the poet sing it with such airs
That one believed he had a sword upstairs;
Yet would be now, could I but have my wish.
Colder and dumber and deafer than a fish.

W. B. YEATS

CHARACTERS

SIR TIMOTHY BELLBOYS
HALLAM MATTHEWS
EDWARD STERNE
A SMALL BOY
LAMPRETT BELLBOYS
DORCAS BELLBOYS
GEORGE SELINCOURT
WILLIAM HUMPAGE
SAMUEL BREEZE
JOSEPH BROTHERHOOD
JAMES GIDDY
RUFUS PIGGOTT
HESTER BELLBOYS
A MAIDSERVANT (PIPPIN)

The scene is the garden before Sir Timothy Bellboys's house in Dorset, on a summer's day in 1804.

ACT ONE – Morning
ACT TWO – Later in the day

A Penny for a Song was first produced at the Theatre Royal, Haymarket, London, on 1 March 1951. It was presented by Tennent Productions Ltd, with the following cast:

WILLIAM HUMPAGE	George Rose
SIR TIMOTHY BELLBOYS	Alan Webb
SAMUEL BREEZE	Denis Cannan
LAMPRETT BELLBOYS	Denys Blakelock
HESTER BELLBOYS	Marie Lohr

HALLAM MATTHEWS	Ronald Squire
DORCAS BELLBOYS	Virginia McKenna
PIPPIN	Joy Rodgers
EDWARD STERNE	Ronald Howard
A SMALL BOY	Derek Rowe
GEORGE SELINCOURT	Basil Radford
JOSEPH BROTHERHOOD	Kenneth Edwards
JAMES GIDDY	Peter Martyn
RUFUS PIGGOTT	Alan Gordon

The play directed by PETER BROOK

A new version of *A Penny for a Song* was presented by the Royal Shakespeare Company at the Aldwych Theatre, London, on 1 August 1962, with the following cast:

WILLIAM HUMPAGE	Newton Blick
SIR TIMOTHY BELLBOYS	Marius Goring
SAMUEL BREEZE	Colin Jeavons
LAMPRETT BELLBOYS	James Bree
HESTER BELLBOYS	Gwen Ffrangcon-Davies
HALLAM MATTHEWS	Michael Gwynn
DORCAS BELLBOYS	Judi Dench
PIPPIN	Margo Andrew
EDWARD STERNE	Mark Eden
A SMALL BOY	Robert Cook
GEORGE SELINCOURT	Clive Morton
JOSEPH BROTHERHOOD	Robert Webber
JAMES GIDDY	Roger Swaine
RUFUS PIGGOTT	Henry Woolf

The play directed by COLIN GRAHAM

ACT ONE

*The scene is the garden before Sir Timothy Bellboys's house in
Dorset. The time is morning of a day in the summer of the year
1804.*

*The garden is bounded on one side by the house: on a second side by
a low wall in which there is a gate leading to an orchard and on
the third side it is open to the sea and sky.*

*At the moment the curtains of the house are drawn but when, later in
the day, they are withdrawn a view is given into a parlour and a
dining-room on the ground floor and of three bedrooms on the first
floor. There is a front door surmounted by an elegant fanlight.
Set about the lawn are various articles of garden furniture.*

*A little apart there is an alcove – a small retreat. This place is
cloistered, self-contained – out of sight of the house and garden.
There is a well: it is fully equipped with windlass and
bucket.*

*The door of the house is closed and the garden is empty but for
WILLIAM HUMPAGE who reclines at a point of vantage in a
tree above the orchard wall. He is asleep and the sun shines down
on his ugly and scarlet face reflecting also in the metal buttons of
his strange uniform: satin knee-breeches with worsted stockings
and boots all surmounted by a gay tunic which is, perhaps, of
some long-forgotten militia. A brass telescope hangs from his hand
and about his wrist is tied a silver whistle. He is surrounded by an
apparatus the purpose of which is not immediately apparent. It
consists of two large wooden flaps or signals – one red, one green
and both movable – the green flap being prominently displayed at
the moment. Also to hand is a great brass bell very highly
polished. It is a fine morning and the sky promises a clear, hot day.*

Suddenly the curtains of a room on the first floor are torn apart and the window is thrown open.

SIR TIMOTHY BELLBOYS, *in a state of partial undress, leans out. After a racking yawn he surveys the garden and beyond with interest. Then, in a frightening voice, he shouts:*

TIMOTHY: Humpage!

HUMPAGE *awakes with a start, scattering several small cakes and the remains of an alfresco meal to the ground. He raises the telescope, in reverse, and putting it to his eye begins to scan seawards with an alarming intensity.*

TIMOTHY *calls again.*

TIMOTHY: Humpage!

HUMPAGE: Sir!

TIMOTHY: Anything to report?

HUMPAGE: No, sir.

TIMOTHY: Nothing in sight?

HUMPAGE: No, sir.

TIMOTHY: No ships?

HUMPAGE: No, sir.

TIMOTHY: No troops?

HUMPAGE: No, sir.

TIMOTHY: Nothing suspicious?

HUMPAGE: No, sir.

TIMOTHY *is about to withdraw.*

TIMOTHY: Were you asleep?

HUMPAGE: No, sir.

TIMOTHY *withdraws to the bedroom and closes the window but does not draw the curtains. He can be seen moving about the room. By this time* SAMUEL BREEZE *has entered the garden.*

He is a servant, neatly dressed: a Londoner by birth. He looks up at HUMPAGE, *who by this time has relaxed.*

BREEZE: 'Morning.

HUMPAGE: 'Morning.

BREEZE: Now this isn't right. I can't seem to find my way around this place at all. I'm looking for the outhouses. (HUMPAGE *points to the back of the house.*) But I've just come that way.

HUMPAGE: Then you must have passed them.

BREEZE: If you say so. I'm a stranger here. However—

BREEZE turns to go back by the way he came and meets LAMPRETT BELLBOYS.

Good morning, sir.

LAMPRETT: Good morning.

BREEZE goes out. At the sight of LAMPRETT, *HUMPAGE is again galvanized into action. He snatches up the telescope and views the countryside.* LAMPRETT *speaks to him.*

Humpage!

HUMPAGE: Sir?

LAMPRETT: Attention! Anything to report?

HUMPAGE: No, sir.

LAMPRETT: Nothing in the night?

HUMPAGE: No, sir.

LAMPRETT: No smoke?

HUMPAGE: No, sir.

LAMPRETT: Oh. (*After a pause.*) Not even a gorse bush?

HUMPAGE: No, sir.

LAMPRETT: Very well, Humpage. Keep your eyes open. Good morning, my love.

He speaks to his wife, HESTER, *who is now standing in the open doorway of the house. She is dressed in clothes of a former period.*

HESTER: Good morning, Lamprett. Have you seen our daughter?

LAMPRETT: No, my dear, I have not.

HESTER (*calls*): Dorcas!

LAMPRETT: Humpage!

HUMPAGE: Sir?

LAMPRETT: Any sight of Miss Bellboys?

HUMPAGE *views about.*

HUMPAGE: No, sir.

HESTER: Tiresome child. Lamprett!

LAMPRETT: My dear?

HESTER: You have on odd shoes. Change them.

She goes into the house. LAMPRETT *sits, removes his shoes and stares at them.*

HUMPAGE: Report, sir!

LAMPRETT (*leaping up*): What's that?

HUMPAGE: Miss Bellboys approaching, sir.

LAMPRETT: Oh. (*He sits again.*)

DORCAS BELLBOYS, *his daughter, runs into the garden.*

Your mother is looking for you, Dorcas.

DORCAS: Why?

LAMPRETT: I don't know. Where have you been?

DORCAS: Swimming.

LAMPRETT: Absurd habit. Your mother tells me my shoes are odd, but I cannot see it. Can you?

Together they examine the shoes.

DORCAS: They seem to be a pair.

LAMPRETT: I think so. However, I'd better change them – you never know.

He goes into the house. DORCAS, *who is barefoot, sits and begins to rub the dry sand from her feet with a handful of grass. Suddenly and simultaneously two bedroom windows are thrown up and* TIMOTHY *and* HESTER *appear.*

HESTER: Dorcas!

TIMOTHY: Humpage!

HESTER: Good morning, Timothy.

TIMOTHY: Good morning, Hester. One moment, please. Humpage!

HUMPAGE: Sir?

TIMOTHY: Which way does the wind blow?

HUMPAGE *produces a small portable wind-vane which he holds in the air.* TIMOTHY *observes this.*

TIMOTHY: That's bad. (*He withdraws.*)

DORCAS: What is it, Mama?

HESTER: How old are you?

DORCAS: Seventeen last birthday.

TIMOTHY *again appears at the window.*

TIMOTHY: Humpage, according to my calculations the wind cannot be blowing from that direction today.

For answer HUMPAGE *again dumbly holds up the vane.*

I see. Then we can expect some excitement. (*He withdraws.*)

HESTER: Seventeen. It has occurred to me that now is the time to put off your childish ways.

DORCAS: Yes, Mama.

HESTER: We must all grow up.

DORCAS: Yes, Mama.

HESTER: Good girl.

HALLAM MATTHEWS *has come from the house.* HALLAM, *a giant of a man, is an exquisite, a dandy par excellence. His clothes are magnificent in their sobriety.*

HALLAM: May I wish you a very good day, Hester?

HESTER: Good morning, Hallam. You're up from your bed, I see.

HALLAM: Indeed, yes. Some time ago. What is that strange noise?

HESTER: The birds of the air, Hallam.

HALLAM: Of course. They sing, don't they?

HESTER: Have you recovered from your journey?

HALLAM: Fully. You remind me: my petulance on arrival last night was unforgivable.

HESTER: I'm sure the looking-glass can be mended. Much more unforgivable was our complete ignorance of your visit. Timothy forgot to tell anyone that you were invited. Have you seen him yet?

HALLAM: I've seen no one but you. Even my man, Breeze. has quite disappeared.

HESTER: Never mind. Nothing in this place is irrevocably lost.

HALLAM: I'm pleased to hear it. But perhaps it had better be known at once – I want peace here, but not complete indifference to my welfare. There was a touch of asperity in that remark, wasn't there? Please forget it.

HESTER: I've done so. There, you're smiling.

HALLAM: Certainly. For today I feel that nothing shall deter me from fully enjoying this charming occupation known as life.

HESTER: How is London?

HALLAM: London, my dear, is hell. I am in disgrace again. Like most men of my age I am in flight, pursued by the agony of love, the danger of war and the misery of democracy. I asked myself: Shall it be a few days in the country with my old friends? I reflected on your peaceful feudalism, far removed from conflict, where love is conducted on the business-like basis of procreation. And a few days in the country it is.

HESTER: We're delighted to have you.

HALLAM: But I'm keeping you from some important duty with my chatter.

HESTER: Good gracious! So you are.

HESTER *goes into the house.* HALLAM *looks about him with appreciation. He sees* HUMPAGE *and decides:*

HALLAM: I think it best, in the circumstances, to ignore you. (*And so, speaks to* DORCAS.) And who are you?

DORCAS: My name is Dorcas.

HALLAM: Ah, yes. The daughter of the house.

DORCAS: Yes.

HALLAM: Charming!

BREEZE, *in a confused state, has wandered into the garden.*

BREEZE: Oh, there you are, Mr Matthews.

HALLAM: Oh, there *you* are, Sam. I think I'm a little angry with you.

BREEZE: Why, sir?

HALLAM: Recall: you left me over an hour ago. In that time I have risen, shaved myself, dressed myself and breakfasted. All this without your usual assistance. Is it right, Sam, is it right?

BREEZE: No, sir. Forgive me.

HALLAM: What have you been doing?

BREEZE: Getting very lost.

HALLAM: Why? The place is simplicity itself – there is the charm.

BREEZE: Have you been that way? (*He indicates the way he has come.*)

HALLAM: Not yet.

BREEZE: I beg of you, sir – don't go that way.

HALLAM: You must not expect every thoroughfare to be as straight as St James's Street. The way about here may be tortuous but the occupants are innocent, honest and homely. Let us absorb these unusual qualities and begin the day. What have you for me this morning?

    BREEZE *takes a book from his pocket.*

BREEZE: Mr William Wordsworth, sir.

HALLAM: Oh, dear! Not a happy choice perhaps, but we must persevere, must we not? And better to have him today in the sunshine than to have him when it is raining. Where shall we take him?

BREEZE: I wouldn't dare to advise you, sir.

HALLAM: In that case we must consult a native of the place. (*He turns to* DORCAS.) Tell me, Dorcas, do you know of a secluded place in the vicinity of this house to which I can retire for a while?

DORCAS: For what purpose?

HALLAM: For the purpose of performing my usual literary chores of the day: which is to have Samuel here read to me from contemporary works. Your expression leads me to understand that you are not fully in sympathy with such an occupation. However, do you know of a suitable place?

DORCAS: I'm trying to think.

HALLAM: Thank you.

DORCAS: There is a ruined cottage on the cliffs.

HALLAM: Excellent! I'd contemplated a field. I'd not dared to hope for a roof.

DORCAS: It has no roof.

HALLAM: No roof. Well, four walls—

DORCAS: Three walls. (*She laughs.*)

HALLAM: I think you are a very nasty little girl. Come, Samuel.

TIMOTHY *appears at the bedroom window.*

TIMOTHY: Hallam! There you are.

HALLAM: Yes, Timothy. Here I am.

TIMOTHY: I shall be down soon to greet you.

HALLAM: That will be very pleasant.

TIMOTHY: Your visit here is secret. (*He puts a finger to his lips.*) Ssh!

HALLAM *replies in the same way.*

Where are you going now?

HALLAM: Just a very little way off, Timothy, for a very little while. Samuel is going to read something new by Mr – what's the fellow's name?

BREEZE: Wordsworth, sir.

HALLAM: By Mr Wordsworth – and I didn't wish to alarm or distress anyone in the house.

TIMOTHY: Well, don't be long. I want to talk to you. (*He is about to withdraw, when:*) Keep your eyes to the south!

HALLAM: I will, indeed.

TIMOTHY *disappears.*

Come, Sam.

HALLAM *goes from the garden followed by* BREEZE. *A diminutive* MAIDSERVANT *can be seen going about within the house withdrawing the curtains of various rooms.*

LAMPRETT *comes from the house.*

LAMPRETT: Who was that?

DORCAS: Matthews and his servant, Sammy.

LAMPRETT: Don't be familiar.

DORCAS: Sorry, Papa.

LAMPRETT: Mr Matthews is a guest here. (*He looks down at his shoes.*) I've changed them.

DORCAS: Have you?

LAMPRETT: Yes. They look better, don't they? This is the uncomfortable pair. Oh, well – to work! Don't dream away the day.

> LAMPRETT *hobbles out.* DORCAS *is now lying full length on the grass.* HUMPAGE *has gone to sleep again. From within the house* HESTER *calls sharply,* Lamprett – Lamprett! *From her recumbent position* DORCAS *slowly raises her legs before her. She regards her feet, flexing her toes, and then, continuing the movement, proceeds to perform a slow backward somersault. This brings her to an inverted view of the orchard gate, where now stand a man and a small boy.*

EDWARD: Very good. Bravo! (*He applauds.*) Do it again.

> DORCAS *gets to her feet: she stares at the man.*

DORCAS: What do you want?

EDWARD: Something to eat and drink.

DORCAS: Are you beggars?

EDWARD: Not really. I could probably render you some small service for the food. Would that make it all right?

DORCAS: No, you can have it for nothing.

EDWARD: Thank you.

> *He stares after* DORCAS *as she rushes headlong into the house.*

> EDWARD STERNE *is a young man of twenty-eight: the small boy is about nine.* EDWARD *looks round the garden. He speaks to the boy.*

EDWARD: This is a very good example of what I was telling you about. The oppression won't strike you at once, but it's there all the same. (*He notices* HUMPAGE.) I see they keep them in trees in these parts. Very original.

TIMOTHY's *bedroom window is thrown up, and* TIMOTHY *leans out.*

TIMOTHY: Humpage!

HUMPAGE (*awakened*): Sir?

TIMOTHY: The portents are ominous.

HUMPAGE *crosses himself.*

Keep your eyes to the south.

HUMPAGE: Yes, sir.

TIMOTHY: Always to the south. (*He notices* EDWARD *and the* BOY.) Good morning to you.

EDWARD: Good morning.

TIMOTHY: A fine morning.

EDWARD: Yes.

TIMOTHY: For a battle, I mean.

He withdraws, closing the window. DORCAS *comes from the house carrying a tray with bread and cheese, some fruit and a tankard.*

DORCAS: This is all I could find.

EDWARD: It looks very nice. Can I eat it here?

DORCAS: If you want to.

EDWARD: Then put it down. (*He throws an apple to the boy, and picks up the tankard.*) What's this?

DORCAS: Beer.

They all sit. EDWARD *and the* BOY *sharing the food and beer.*

EDWARD: My name's Edward Sterne.

DORCAS: How do you do. I'm Dorcas Bellboys. Can you make a living this way?

EDWARD: It's as honest as any other way.

DORCAS: I didn't say it wasn't. I just asked if it was possible.

EDWARD: I don't know yet. I've only just started.

DORCAS: Have you come far?

EDWARD: About a thousand miles.

DORCAS: How far?

EDWARD: About a thousand miles. Is this local cheese?

DORCAS: What? Yes.

EDWARD: It's very good. (*To the* BOY.) Isn't it?
> *The* BOY *nods his head.*

(*To* DORCAS.) I was a soldier. A mercenary.

DORCAS: I don't know what that means.

EDWARD: It means that I got paid for it. I was with the Austrian army. Then two or three years ago, after Hohen-linden – that was a battle: we lost it – I started for home. We've had to take our time. (*He stares up at* HUMPAGE.) When I left England they used to keep the servants under-foot.

DORCAS (*she follows his look*): I don't know what you're talking about.

EDWARD: I'm talking about social inequality.

DORCAS: I've never heard of it. (*Pause.*) I'm very sorry.

EDWARD: It doesn't matter. Is there any more to eat?

DORCAS: No.

EDWARD: Do you mind if I smoke?

DORCAS: Not at all. Are you going far?
> EDWARD *takes out a pipe, and begins to fill and light it.*

EDWARD: To London.

DORCAS: Just for pleasure?

EDWARD: I don't do anything just for pleasure.

DORCAS: You should.

EDWARD: Where have you lived all your life?

DORCAS: Here.

EDWARD: Has it been a useful existence? Has it? So far?

DORCAS: Well, I . . .

EDWARD: Have you subscribed?

DORCAS: I've tried to be a good girl.

EDWARD: That's got nothing to do with it! Look – what's your name?

DORCAS: Dorcas.

EDWARD: Look, Dorcas, the world's full of people. Yes?

DORCAS: I suppose so.

EDWARD: Believe me, it is. And they live in many different

states of power and weakness, wealth and poverty. Right?

DORCAS: Er, yes.

EDWARD: There was a revolution in France, and there's been one in America.

DORCAS: Yes, it was very shocking.

EDWARD: You are a silly girl! It wasn't shocking, it was perfectly splendid. Now, say after me: Revolution is a good thing.

DORCAS (*after a moment*): Revolution is a good thing.

EDWARD: All my kind must go down before the scythe of history.

DORCAS: All my kind must go down before the scythe of history.

EDWARD (*he points at* HUMPAGE): That man will triumph in the end.

DORCAS: No, no, I'm sorry. But I very much doubt it.

EDWARD: You have little faith for one so young.

DORCAS: But, apart from the war, aren't things all right as they are?

EDWARD (*he stares at her; then*): Is there any more beer?

    DORCAS *shakes her head.* TIMOTHY *appears at his window.*

TIMOTHY: Dorcas!

DORCAS: Yes?

TIMOTHY: Is Mr Matthews back?

DORCAS: No.

TIMOTHY: Ask him to come up to me when he returns.

DORCAS: Very well.

TIMOTHY: And remember—

DORCAS: To keep my eyes to the south.

TIMOTHY: That's right. (*To* EDWARD.) And you, sir – all eyes to the south.

    TIMOTHY *withdraws.*

EDWARD: Why to the south?

DORCAS: Because it's from that way Bonaparte will come. They say he'll come with his armies any day now. He's been preparing for months, and – well, look at the weather.

EDWARD: Yes, I'd say it's a very good day for a battle, although from my experience almost any kind of day will do. What do you know of the social and political causes of this war?

DORCAS: Nothing.

EDWARD: But you're prepared to fight it?

DORCAS: Isn't everybody? Why do you look at me like that? There's not much I could do, anyway.

EDWARD: You're a very interesting example of your kind.

DORCAS (*delighted*): Am I? Am I, really?

EDWARD: And so, I expect, are all the people here. Who was that?

He nods towards TIMOTHY's *window.*

DORCAS: My uncle Timothy.

EDWARD: What's he up to?

DORCAS: He's getting ready to defeat Napoleon.

EDWARD: Single-handed?

DORCAS: Yes.

EDWARD: I see. Are you an orphan?

DORCAS: No. Why?

EDWARD: I thought, living here alone with your uncle—

DORCAS: I don't live here alone with him. There's Mama and Papa as well. And—

EDWARD: What do they do?

DORCAS: Well, Mama looks after the house—

EDWARD: But what does your father do?

DORCAS: Nothing much.

EDWARD: Exactly.

DORCAS: He looks after his fire-engine—

EDWARD: His what?

DORCAS: His fire-engine. He loves it very much.

EDWARD: It's not enough, Dorcas.

LAMPRETT *appears from behind the house.*

LAMPRETT: Dorcas.

DORCAS: Yes, Papa?

LAMPRETT: I beg your pardon. Do I disturb you? Good morning.

EDWARD: Good morning.

LAMPRETT (*seeing the* SMALL BOY): Ah! Little boy. You'll do. Come with me.

> *The* BOY *hesitates.*

DORCAS: Go with him. He won't hurt you. He's my father.

> *The* SMALL BOY *gets up and slowly crosses the garden to* LAMPRETT, *who takes him by the arm: together they go out.*

EDWARD: I don't know how he'll get on.

DORCAS: The little boy?

EDWARD: Yes. He doesn't speak much English.

DORCAS: Why not?

EDWARD: Because he's French.

DORCAS: What are you doing together? I thought you fought the French.

EDWARD: I did.

DORCAS: I thought we were supposed to be fighting them now.

EDWARD: We are.

DORCAS: But that boy—

EDWARD: Funny things get left on a battlefield. It's mostly rubbish, small change. Bodies, equipment, uneaten food, animals – I remember I found it queer when the birds didn't stop singing during the firing – that sort of thing. A man picks up what he can when the fighting's done. Some are luckier than others. I got lumbered with that kid.

DORCAS: How?

EDWARD: Well, he was there. Like me. History pushes our kind around. He was conceived, born and brought up for the first six years of his life in a waggon. Then at 'Linden his father was killed, and his mother ran off with a quartermaster. Peace was signed and we were all told to go home.

But his home was upturned in a ditch. So we started walking.

DORCAS: You saved him.

EDWARD: No, he was loot.

DORCAS: You helped him.

EDWARD: I just found him, that's all.

HESTER, *within the house, calls:* Dorcas – Dorcas!

DORCAS: Oh, she'll want something. Perhaps to send you away. Come on.

She takes EDWARD *by the hand, and they go.* HESTER *comes from the house. She looks about the garden and then calls:*

HESTER: Lamprett!

HUMPAGE *awakes and views the horizon through his telescope.* LAMPRETT *comes into the garden.*

LAMPRETT: I've changed them, my dear.

HESTER: Changed what?

LAMPRETT: My shoes.

HESTER: Never mind that now. What are you doing?

LAMPRETT: Cleaning the engine.

HESTER: Again?

LAMPRETT: Well, my dear—

HESTER: You cleaned it only yesterday.

LAMPRETT: We must be prepared.

HESTER: Ridiculous!

LAMPRETT *prepares to go.*

Lamprett!

LAMPRETT: My dear?

HESTER: Do I bully you?

LAMPRETT (*he smiles*): A little.

HESTER (*she smiles*): Forgive me. I must a little or belie my appearance.

LAMPRETT: Of course.

HESTER: Have you seen Dorcas?

LAMPRETT: A moment ago.

HESTER: Where?

LAMPRETT: I really can't remember.

HESTER: She's growing up, Lamprett.

LAMPRETT: Yes, with a young man.

HESTER: What's that?

LAMPRETT: I saw her with a young man.

HESTER: You see! (*She turns to go into the house.*)

LAMPRETT: Hester—

HESTER: Yes?

LAMPRETT: Did you wish to speak to me?

HESTER: I don't think so.

LAMPRETT: You called me as if you wished to speak to me.

HESTER: Then what can I say? (*She pauses.*) God bless you. (*She goes into the house.*)

LAMPRETT: Humpage!

HUMPAGE: Sir!

LAMPRETT: If this fellow, Napoleon Bonaparte, does come over with an army I expect there will be work to do. The battle is sure to start a few fires. Murder, rapine, looting – that sort of thing, you know.

HUMPAGE: Yes, sir.

LAMPRETT: It will, however—

As LAMPRETT *continues to speak, the* BOY *comes in to hand him a polishing rag.*

– be more difficult than usual – thank you, my dear –

The BOY *returns to his duties.*

– considerably more difficult. For while we must extinguish our own fires we must be careful to foster those of the enemy.

HUMPAGE: That's right, sir.

LAMPRETT: There our duty as Englishmen must precede our duty as firemen. But knowing how against the grain it will be to foster – indeed, positively encourage! – any fire, friend's or enemy's, I've been considering the advisability of using some combustible mixture in certain hoses. Have you anything to suggest?

HUMPAGE: Brandy.

LAMPRETT: Well, yes—

> HALLAM MATTHEWS, *followed by* BREEZE, *enters the garden.*

HALLAM: Take those things to my room, Samuel. I shall sit here for a while.

> BREEZE *goes into the house.* HALLAM *sits down, fanning himself.*

HALLAM: Good morning, Lamprett.

LAMPRETT: Good morning, Hallam.

HALLAM: Inflammatory weather.

LAMPRETT: Yes, thank God. Have you been walking?

HALLAM: Yes. Your daughter—

> BREEZE *re-enters the garden. He carries a small jewelled box which he hands to* HALLAM.

BREEZE: Your lozenges, sir.

HALLAM: Oh, thank you, Sam.

> BREEZE *goes back into the house.*

For my voice, you know. Have one – delicious.

LAMPRETT: No thank you. Been walking, have you?

HALLAM: Yes. Your daughter advised me of a secluded place to which I could retire for the purpose of reading.

LAMPRETT: Excellent!

HALLAM: It was far from excellent. The premises themselves had little to commend them other than an overpowering smell of decaying seaweed, a complete exposure of the sky, and the fact that they were situated on a sheer precipice of several hundred feet. You must know, my dear Lamprett, that nothing is so necessary to a reading of Mr Wordsworth's work as a sense of security.

LAMPRETT: Reading that fellow, eh?

HALLAM: It was my intention. I must attempt to know something of the forces that are conspiring the destruction of my kind.

LAMPRETT: Where was this place?

HALLAM: A ruined cottage – in that direction.

LAMPRETT: Oh, that place.

HALLAM: You know it?

LAMPRETT: Yes. It was burnt out two years ago – a magnificent conflagration! – the only occasion on which my brigade became sea-borne. An unfortunate legend credits me with firing the place – it was the first time my brigade was called out under my captaincy – but I can assure you it is nothing more than a legend. (*He points to* HUMPAGE.) He used to live there.

HALLAM: Now he lives up there?

LAMPRETT: Yes. He's the look-out.

HALLAM: And what does he look out for?

LAMPRETT: Fires. Any spark, flash, flame or cloud of smoke as small as a man's hand and I am instantly informed. The engine stands ready – the signals and bell are a summons to the members of my brigade. We should proceed within seconds.

HALLAM: Excellent!

LAMPRETT: I believe Timothy also employs Humpage as a look-out for any sign of this threatened invasion but that is a secondary consideration. Have you seen Timothy yet?

HALLAM: For a moment. He called to me from his window.

LAMPRETT: I think I should tell you, Hallam, that you will find him strange – very strange. God forbid that I should speak ill of my brother—

HALLAM: God forbid!

LAMPRETT: – but this threatened invasion by Bonaparte seems to have unhinged him completely. His behaviour has become eccentric in the extreme.

    HUMPAGE, *in his active viewing of the surrounding country-side, turns and lightly strikes the brass bell with the telescope.* LAMPRETT *leaps to his feet.*

LAMPRETT: Action!

HUMPAGE: An accident, sir. It was an accident. (*He demonstrates.*) I was viewing about as is my duty, and the bell being in this position – here – my arm raised – so – I accidentally struck the bell – so! (*He does so.*) An accident, sir. See? If my arm is raised – so – and I am viewing – so – I am able—

He again strikes the bell. Then there is silence. At last LAMPRETT *speaks.*

LAMPRETT: A false alarm.

HUMPAGE: Yes, sir.

LAMPRETT: No fire.

HUMPAGE: No, sir.

LAMPRETT: No smoke.

HUMPAGE: No, sir.

LAMPRETT: In fact, nothing.

HUMPAGE: Nothing, sir.

LAMPRETT (*shouting*): That is no excuse for relaxation! Attention!

HUMPAGE *again takes up the telescope and begins to view with an insane concentration.*

LAMPRETT: You were saying, Hallam?—

HALLAM: I wasn't saying anything. You were speaking of Timothy.

LAMPRETT: Of course. Quite unhinged, poor fellow. Given to the most extraordinary outbursts and madcap schemes. Very sad to see a man of his capabilities with his reason overthrown. My brother – very sad.

HALLAM: Yes, indeed. But the cause surely is not—

LAMPRETT: Nothing more than this absurd invasion by the French. He has no trust in the official precautions in hand against Bonaparte.

HALLAM: By that he shows his sanity.

LAMPRETT: You mean—

HALLAM: I mean that any system of national defence is non-existent.

LAMPRETT: God bless my soul!

HALLAM: However, what is Timothy proposing to do?

LAMPRETT: I thought you must know. I had imagined you were in his confidence.

HALLAM: I know nothing more than this: that I am arrived from London by Timothy's wish and bring him a box of clothes and a French phrase book.

LAMPRETT: A box of clothes and a French phrase book! My God, what can he be up to?

HALLAM: We shall just have to wait and see, my dear Lamprett, just wait and see.

LAMPRETT: That is a notion to which I have never subscribed. I find out, my dear Hallam, I find out!

HALLAM: Then pray tell me – what have you found out?

LAMPRETT: Nothing.

HALLAM: Nothing. I see.

LAMPRETT: Except that his room is hung with maps and reports of the weather – that he has set four mantraps in the orchard – that I was awakened three nights ago by his calling out words of command in a foreign language – except for these things I know nothing.

At this moment TIMOTHY *appears in the doorway of the house. He is now fully dressed and carries a pistol. This he raises and aims at the brass bell. He fires and the bell chimes under the impact of the bullet.*

TIMOTHY: Good shot, sir! Sit down, Lamprett. (*He exhibits the pistol.*) Hit a penny at ten paces last night. Pretended it was Boney's belly-button. Good morning, Hallam.

HALLAM: Good morning, Timothy.

TIMOTHY: A brisk and beautiful day!

HALLAM: Indeed, yes.

TIMOTHY: Have a good journey?

HALLAM: Very fair.

TIMOTHY: Sorry I was not available to welcome you. What time did you arrive?

HALLAM: A little past midnight.

TIMOTHY: Sleep well?

HALLAM: Thank you, yes.

TIMOTHY: Breakfasted?

HALLAM: Yes.

TIMOTHY: Well, that's done.

HALLAM: What, pray, is done?

TIMOTHY: The conventional inquiries as to your general welfare. Tedious, eh? Now, I want to talk to you. Off with you, Lamprett.

LAMPRETT: What's that?

TIMOTHY: I say, off with you. I want to speak to Hallam privately.

LAMPRETT: Oh, very well.

TIMOTHY: Now, Hallam. I wish to tell you about a little plan. That is, when Lamprett has had the decency to absent himself.

He glares at LAMPRETT, *who is hanging about the house.*

LAMPRETT: Timothy.

TIMOTHY: Yes.

LAMPRETT: Where can I go? What can I do?

TIMOTHY: God bless my soul! Our very existence is threatened by Napoleon Bonaparte, and the man asks where he can go and what he can do. Prepare, my dear brother, prepare for the worst in whatever way you please – but prepare.

LAMPRETT: I think you are a very foolish fellow, Tim.

He leaves the garden with a certain dignity. TIMOTHY *stares after him.*

TIMOTHY: I am being made to understand with increasing force the impossibility of expecting Lamprett to take his life with the smallest degree of seriousness. He has, I'm afraid, an incontrovertibly frivolous nature. Father, had he lived, would have found an even deeper dissatisfaction with his younger son, I feel. During his lifetime he found Lamprett a sore trial. We cannot deny that the affair of Hester whilst Lamprett was at Oxford—

HALLAM: Hester! His wife!

TIMOTHY: Oh, yes, he married her. Father insisted upon it – and quite rightly – after the disgraceful business of the warden's breeches. Hester was his niece, you know.

HALLAM: I didn't know.

TIMOTHY: Lamprett, of course, has lived in complete retirement ever since. His passions must be controlled.

HALLAM: Lamprett's passions!

TIMOTHY: No, no! You misunderstand me. I mean, of course, his passion for lost causes. That is how the disgrace came upon us. Instead of attending to his studies when he was at Oxford he became convinced that women should be admitted to the Colleges. To prove their worth he prevailed upon Hester – with whom he was friendly, both of them playing the bass fiddle – to dress in her uncle's second-best ceremonial breeches and coat. So dressed, she attended lectures for three weeks and might never have been discovered had not Lamprett then insisted that to complete the illusion she should begin to smoke. One evening, in his rooms, with Horace Walpole as his guest, Hester was standing before the fire, pipe in hand, when the breeches caught alight. She would have been burnt to the ground had not Lamprett extinguished the fire manually. (*He demonstrates.*) So, of course, he married her, and he's been fighting fires ever since. As for the present – I can only enjoin you to the greatest secrecy.

HALLAM: We are not alone.

He indicates HUMPAGE.

TIMOTHY: Very true. Humpage!

HUMPAGE: Sir!

TIMOTHY: You are not to listen to my conversation for the next few minutes. Do you understand?

HUMPAGE: Very good, sir. (*He covers his ears with his hands.*)

TIMOTHY: No, no, no! You must keep your ears open for other sounds! The approach of danger may be heralded by nothing more than a whisper, the advance of an army may be borne on the gentlest breeze. Take down your hands!

   HUMPAGE *remains covering his ears: he grins.*
Take down your hands!

   HUMPAGE *does not move.*
God grant me patience! (TIMOTHY *shouts.*) Listen, you blockhead! Listen!

   He then stands silent and at a complete loss until, in a moment of inspiration, he snatches off his hat and throws it to HUMPAGE *who, with an automatic reaction, catches it.* TIMOTHY *seizes the opportunity.*

TIMOTHY: Listen! You are to keep your eyes open for other sounds, but you are not to listen to me. Do you understand?

HUMPAGE: Yes, sir.

TIMOTHY: Keep your eyes to the south – and give me back my hat.

   HUMPAGE *does so.*
(*to* HALLAM) Sorry about that. To continue, I must, as I say, énjoin you to the greatest secrecy. It is a well-known fact that this part of the coast is alive with French spies and Bonaparte's personal agents. Now, have I your solemn word that you will not tell a single living soul?

HALLAM: I can give you my word on that with the greatest assurance.

TIMOTHY: Thank you. You have brought me some things from London.

HALLAM: Yes.

TIMOTHY: What are they?

HALLAM: A large black box which you asked me to collect from Drury Lane Theatre—

TIMOTHY: Where is it?

HALLAM: Upstairs in my room.

TIMOTHY: Hidden?

HALLAM: Under the bed.

TIMOTHY: Locked?

HALLAM: Locked.

TIMOTHY: And the second article?

HALLAM: This book – (*He takes it from his pocket.*) – which appears to be—

TIMOTHY: Excellent! (*He takes the book from* HALLAM *and reads in execrable French.*) *Sautons à bas du lit, j'entends la bonne qui monte.* Dear me! I'm not sure this is the sort of thing I want at all. (*He turns a few pages.*) Ah! This is better. (*He reads.*) *Retirez! Je connais le dessous des cartes!*

HALLAM: What does that mean?

TIMOTHY *consults the book.*

TIMOTHY: 'Retreat! I know what's what!' Oh, yes – I think I shall find what I want in here. It will repay a few hours' quiet study. Good. (*He puts the book away in his pocket.*) Now, Hallam. The situation is roughly this: myself, versus one hundred and seventy-five thousand Frenchmen.

HALLAM: An epic situation, no less. Go on.

TIMOTHY: That is the popular estimate of the number of Bonaparte's troops assembled on the French coast at this moment, and preparing for the final assault. They will make the crossing in two thousand shallops, dispatch boats, caques, bomb-ships, praams and transports. That crossing may be made at any moment now. What is to be done?

HALLAM: What, indeed?

TIMOTHY: I'll tell you in a moment. But first let us consider the arrangements made by the country as a whole to deal with this menace. Are they daring, brilliant and worthy of the English in such a situation? Are they?

HALLAM: I should say, no.

TIMOTHY: And you would be right. Shall I tell you why they are not daring, brilliant and worthy of the English?

HALLAM: If you please.

TIMOTHY: Because they do not exist. No arrangements for dealing with this menace exist.

HALLAM: Astounding!

TIMOTHY: Disgraceful! A national disgrace! But you will agree that something must be done.

HALLAM: I should think so.

TIMOTHY: Well, what?

HALLAM: You are aching to tell me, Timothy.

TIMOTHY: My first plan was to raise a private army under my command. I actually put this plan into action. Two months ago I raised a force of one hundred and twenty-seven men – eight children: the Bellboys Fencibles. All was prepared, the corps was in being, when I received a communication from some central office in Dorchester informing me that the raising of an army for a private purpose – my God! a private purpose – was illegal. More than that, I was also informed that owing to the national emergency, my corps – the Bellboys Fencibles – would be taken over intact. I applied, very naturally, for their command. It was refused. Can you credit that?

HALLAM: With difficulty.

TIMOTHY: Yes, refused. But – and this will strain your credulity to breaking-point – I was informed that an officer was being sent from Taunton to take up the command and that they wished me – my God! I can hardly tell you – they wished me to give him any advice and information on the corps and local terrain that he desired.

HALLAM: Which you have undoubtedly done.

TIMOTHY: Nothing of the kind. I refused even to meet the fellow. I withdrew my support and every material object associating me with the corps – including the banners bearing the corps inscription – 'Tintinnabulum pueri'. I washed my hands of them.

HALLAM: Understandably.

TIMOTHY: This Taunton fellow – what's his name? – George

Selincourt – has had them in training now for almost two months, and if you should chance upon a ragged band of scruffy, drunken, ill-disciplined, noisy louts rampaging the countryside you will be viewing our sole defence against Bonaparte.

HALLAM: Alarming!

TIMOTHY: Something, however, must be done. You agree?

HALLAM: Yes.

TIMOTHY: It will be done. Never fear.

HALLAM: You have a plan.

TIMOTHY: I have. (*He smiles in anticipation.*) You will understand that in such a situation a gesture of defiance is useless. The odds are great.

HALLAM: One hundred and seventy-five thousand to one, you said.

TIMOTHY: Yes.

HALLAM: I think those odds may be considered as lunatic.

TIMOTHY: Quite. Therefore, as I say, a direct conflict must be avoided. Yet I contemplate engaging the French single-handed, using but a single weapon.

HALLAM: The jawbone of an ass, I presume.

TIMOTHY *rises to stand a little apart from* HALLAM. *He pulls a lock of hair down over his forehead and stands squeezing his cheek with his right hand.*

TIMOTHY: I am a certain person making a grand decision of policy.

HALLAM: How many guesses am I allowed?

TIMOTHY: Oh, come, come! Only one should be necessary.

HALLAM *is silent.*

I'll give you a clue. (*He then says, in his very individual French:*) *Mettez bas les armes! Vive la France!*

HALLAM: *Comme vous écorchez cette langue!*

TIMOTHY: I beg your pardon?

HALLAM: Nothing.

TIMOTHY: You understand who I am?

HALLAM: You know, I'm very much afraid that I do. But I don't see—

TIMOTHY: You must see! The resemblance is remarkable, you will admit. I can look very like Napoleon Bonaparte, and there lies the basis of my scheme of defeat for the French. At the moment the likeness is possibly remote, but when I am dressed—

HALLAM: Dressed?

TIMOTHY: Exactly! The box that you have brought for me contains a uniform of the French National Guard.

HALLAM: My God!

TIMOTHY: And here is my plan. I shall be informed of the approach of the French fleet, the moment of imminent invasion. At that moment I shall do nothing – nothing! I shall allow the army to disembark, to land on the coast out there. I shall not make the slightest effort to prevent them from doing so. When their landing is almost complete I shall dress in the National Guard uniform and assume my impersonation of Bonaparte. I shall then descend the well. I shall have to be lowered in the bucket. Perhaps you would be so good as to oblige me—

HALLAM *inclines his head in assent.*

I shall then make my way along the tunnel at the bottom of the well which leads to the cliffs, and I shall make an appearance behind – mark this! – I shall come up in the rear of the French army. They will, of course, recognize me as their Emperor and consent to be led by me.

HALLAM: And where, pray, do you intend to lead them?

TIMOTHY: To confusion and ultimate damnation!

HALLAM: How?

TIMOTHY: I shall give orders. Inform them that all is lost: that there is nothing but retreat.

HALLAM: In their own language?

TIMOTHY: Certainly. That is why I required this little book. (*He pats his pocket.*) I know a certain amount, of course.

Je suis l'avant-coureur! Je suis l'Empereur! – and that sort of thing. (*For a moment he regards* HALLAM *with a smile – then:*) Well, what do you think of it?

HALLAM: I am really at a loss for words.

TIMOTHY: The charm – the essential charm of the plan is its simplicity, eh?

HALLAM: Yes – yes.

TIMOTHY: Can I have the key to the box of clothes?

HALLAM: In my room, on the dressing-table.

TIMOTHY: Thank you. (*He turns to go into the house.*) I may fail – but what of that? It is what we attempt that matters. I know by your sympathetic reception that I am right at least in the attempt. I can even forgive the desperate foolishness of my fellow-countrymen. Alas! They cannot comprehend what is almost upon them. But I will stand for them. I will be England. I shall now retire for a while. A little study, you know.

He pats the book in his pocket, laughs, and then goes into the house. HALLAM *turns to* DORCAS *and* EDWARD, *who are now standing at the gateway of the orchard.*

HALLAM: Hullo, horrid child.

DORCAS: Mr Matthews. (*A deep curtsy.*) May I introduce Mr Edward Sterne to your acquaintance.

HALLAM: How do you do. I've just had a very exhausting time with your uncle. So do you think you could find me somewhere to sit?

DORCAS: What about here?

HALLAM: Yes, that looks all right. Is it dry?

DORCAS: Yes.

HALLAM: Thank you. (*He sits down.*) The country has a bad effect on my manservant. It seems to swallow him up all the time.

EDWARD: Which means you have to do things for yourself.

HALLAM: Yes. Tiresome, isn't it?

EDWARD: No.

HALLAM: I beg your pardon?

EDWARD: It's very good for you.

HALLAM: Oh, my God! Who are you?

EDWARD: I'm not any man's servant.

DORCAS: Mr Sterne believes in democracy.

HALLAM: We all believe in it, my dear, but some of us are too well-mannered to practise it.

EDWARD: What will you do when the time comes and you can't get anybody to serve you?

HALLAM: I can answer that quite simply. I shall die of neglect.

DORCAS (to EDWARD): He's the kind you meant when you said their passing would be like the melting of snow to show the promise of spring beneath, isn't he?

HALLAM: Not only a radical, but a poetical radical. (*He calls.*) Sam!

EDWARD: There's some good to be said for them.

DORCAS: Is there?

EDWARD: Yes. Their supreme selfishness provides the rock against which we can break ourselves.

DORCAS: Oh, you're marvellous! Isn't he, Mr Matthews?

HALLAM: No. Dorcas, does your mother or father know that you are acquainted with this gentleman?

DORCAS: Not really.

HALLAM: Then listen to me, Mr Sterne. This child is the daughter of a very old friend of mine. I was at school with her uncle—

EDWARD: Which school?

HALLAM: Never mind which school. You'll only throw it in my face. What I'm trying to say is this: She has been well brought up according to tried and tested ideas. You might say that she is a traditional child, and none the worse for that. I want you to think very carefully before you put these ideas in her head, ideas which are far below her station. The opportunities for revolution are few in this charming place. It would be sad, I think you'll agree, if you

were to leave behind a convert with no material to work
on.

EDWARD: Typical.

HALLAM: I'm sure I am.

EDWARD: You safeguard your own tottering position by
chatter about tradition. This girl has a right to her own life.
You make her look very small by taking it for granted that
she wants to live in your way. She may have a conscience:
have you thought of that? She may be ashamed to build her
folly, as you do, on the labour of the poor.

HALLAM: You're quite wrong. My money doesn't come
from the sweat of the poor. I get it by gambling, and loans
from friends. It's all perfectly respectable.

There is silence. DORCAS *looks from one to the other.*

DORCAS: Do go on.

HALLAM (*to* EDWARD): Your turn.

EDWARD: For the last four years I've been walking about
Europe. I've seen such horrible things that it broke my
heart. Poverty and disease, love and friendship ruined by
war, men and women living like animals in a desperate
attempt to stay alive. I was one who sold himself for war so
that he could eat, and I've had women sell themselves to me
so that their children could eat. Now I may be simple,
Matthews, but there's cause for all this. And the cause is
laziness and indifference. There are only a handful of
tyrants at any one time, but there are millions who don't
care. I saw all this, I smelt it, I lay down with it at night,
and at last I decided to fight. I carried in my pocket a book
which is a weapon. It has a title which will mean nothing
to you. It's called *The Rights of Man.*

Silence.

HALLAM: That was most unfair. You were serious.

EDWARD: I'm afraid I was. I'm sorry.

HALLAM: May I bring the discussion back to a more accept-
able level?

EDWARD: Please do.

HALLAM: Very well. Don't address me as if I were a society, Mr Sterne. I am a private individual. One of the few remaining in England.

EDWARD: What does that mean?

HALLAM: I'll tell you. I live my own life. I don't try to live other people's lives for them, nor do I ask that they should live mine. I like the world very much as it is. As for subscribing to it, I suppose it is true that I give little. The most that can be said for me is that I attempt to decorate it. I try to write poetry, and fail. I have published three polemical pamphlets on quite uncontroversial subjects. I belong to one or two decent clubs, but no societies. I have read your Thomas Paine and Jeremy Bentham and Rousseau, not on a public platform, but in the privacy of my library. It is both wrong and dangerous, Mr Sterne, to think that the disagreement of my kind with your kind is based on ignorance. I am a Tory in politics, and a kind of Christian. And now, having made that bid for unpopularity, perhaps the war had better begin.

DORCAS: And what do you think of war, Mr Matthews?

HALLAM: I dislike it. A noisy and untidy business.

DORCAS: Have you had much experience of it?

HALLAM: I was in the army for five years.

EDWARD: Why did you leave?

HALLAM: I—

DORCAS: You resigned in protest.

HALLAM: No, I—

DORCAS: You couldn't stand the brutality of it all.

HALLAM: You're really too kind. Actually I—

DORCAS: The sight of blood revolted you.

HALLAM: Hush, darling. Actually, it was the food. I found it too disgusting for words. And I was expected to keep the most extraordinary hours.

DORCAS: Oh.

HALLAM: You're not going to fall in love with me, Dorcas, so I can admit acting from prejudice, and not principle. Take her away, Mr Sterne, and complete the conversion. It's a lovely day for it.

EDWARD (*to* DORCAS): Shall we go?

DORCAS: Yes.

> DORCAS *and* EDWARD *go, leaving* HALLAM *staring after them.* HESTER *comes from the house.*

HESTER (*to* HALLAM): Don't sit in the sun!

> HESTER *returns to the house, passing* BREEZE, *who is coming out into the garden.* HALLAM *sees* BREEZE.

HALLAM: Ah, Sam!

BREEZE: You seem very relieved to see me, sir. Anything the matter?

HALLAM: I'm a little upset, Sam, that's all. But you're happy, I see. Enjoying yourself?

BREEZE: Very much, thank you, sir. Nothing like a few days in the country, is there?

HALLAM: Nothing like it in the whole wide world, I should think.

BREEZE: I say, you are in a state.

HALLAM: Yes, I am, quite decidedly, in a state. It's the young people, Sam, with their passion for causes. Most of them lost.

BREEZE: I don't like to see you in such a way. I leave you happily talking about yourself. I come back to find you in a state. From past experience I'd say that people here are either paying too much attention to you, or too little. Has someone suggested that you're either too young or too old?

HALLAM: Sam, I beg you, don't let the young man who is with Miss Bellboys into the kitchen.

BREEZE: All right, sir.

HALLAM: Or I shall probably find a tricolour stuck in my pudding.

BREEZE: Contain yourself, sir.

HALLAM: Tell me, Sam, are you fond of me?

BREEZE: I'm devoted to you, sir.

HALLAM: You've never felt like blowing me up, or burning me down?

BREEZE: Certainly not.

HALLAM: You may as well. For the young people speak, and I am revealed – a magnificent ruin!

BREEZE: Then if I may say so, sir, it's not going to do you any good walking up and down like that.

HALLAM: Am I walking up and down? God help me! (*He sinks into a chair.*)

BREEZE: I think we can find you something more comfortable than that. (*He looks around the garden and sees the alcove.*) Ah! What about this? (*He goes into the alcove.*) It feels to be dry and warm. You need not necessarily sleep, sir. Will you go in?

HALLAM: I am tempted, I confess.

Suddenly they smile at each other.

BREEZE: Come along, sir.

HALLAM *goes into the alcove.*

Put your feet up.

HALLAM *sitting, does so.*

I think it would be wise to remove your hat. Ah! This is useful. (*He has discovered a shawl.*) Put it round your shoulders.

HALLAM *drapes himself.*

Is the light going to bother you? It's rather strong.

HALLAM *looks doubtful.*

Cover your face, sir. (*He takes* HALLAM's *handkerchief and puts it over his face.*)

HALLAM: Is it necessary?

BREEZE: Let it be a little curtain between you and the world. Out here, vulgar mankind – behind there, Boodles. How's that? Now you can forget your troubles, can't you. (*He begins to tiptoe away.*)

HALLAM: Where are you going?

BREEZE: To the orchard, sir.

HALLAM: What have you got in that orchard?

BREEZE: Some apples—

HALLAM: Yes?

BREEZE: A pint of cider—

HALLAM: Yes?

BREEZE: And a young woman named Chastity Meadows.

HALLAM: Off you go.

BREEZE: Thank you, sir.

He goes out to the orchard. HALLAM *turns restlessly beneath the handkerchief and shawl.* HUMPAGE *has again fallen asleep.* LAMPRETT *and the* BOY *enter in earnest conversation. The* BOY *carries a large home-made firework of complicated design.*

LAMPRETT: – and I cannot impress upon you enough the vital necessity of placing that apparatus under – mark that! under – the object. The reason for this is the blow-back which might – and this is no exaggeration – decapitate you. (*He crouches beside the* BOY *over the firework.*) My experiments with fire-fighting by explosives are in a primitive state as yet, but we progress. This is the fuzee with which I set it off – this is a linstock. Both technical terms you will learn in due course. Now – ready? When I have lit it we will retire to a safe distance. (*He applies the fuzee to the firework and cries:*) Right!

He and the BOY *rush from the garden. For a time there is stillness, then the firework goes off. It is dazzling, but quite silent. The* BOY *and* LAMPRETT *return.* LAMPRETT *explains.*

I am putting the sound in it later. In my opinion, the only way of extinguishing a fire is to blow up – well, everything that is burning if necessary. The loss of life would probably be considerable, but we must keep in mind the main object – and that is, to put out the fire.

LAMPRETT *and the* BOY *go out to the orchard.* GEORGE SELINCOURT *enters with considerable energy. He is a little upset at finding the garden apparently deserted. Suddenly, from within a room on the first floor of the house,* TIMOTHY *shouts.*

TIMOTHY: Bravo! *Cours, cours et cours encore!*

SELINCOURT: Foreigners!

HUMPAGE (*he is asleep*): Yes.

SELINCOURT: Bless me!

Looking up at HUMPAGE, *he moves across the garden until he comes to rest, at a complete loss, just above the alcove where* HALLAM MATTHEWS *lies. After a moment* HALLAM *speaks.*

HALLAM: Are you by any chance a French spy?

SELINCOURT: Good God! (*He discovers* HALLAM.) What did you say?

HALLAM: I asked if, by any chance, you were a French spy.

SELINCOURT: Certainly not!

HALLAM: Not?

SELINCOURT: No.

During the following conversation HALLAM *does not move or take the handkerchief from his face.*

SELINCOURT: Excuse me—

HALLAM: Yes?

SELINCOURT: Would you be Sir Timothy Bellboys?

HALLAM: My dear sir, I wouldn't be Sir Timothy Bellboys for all the tea in China.

SELINCOURT: No, no! You misunderstand me. I mean, of course, are you Sir Timothy Bellboys?

HALLAM: No.

SELINCOURT: Not?

HALLAM: No.

SELINCOURT: That is a pity.

HALLAM: On the contrary, sir, it is a stroke of fortune for which I have never ceased to thank Providence.

SELINCOURT: My name is George Selincourt. (*There is silence.*) Selincourt. (*He spells it.*)

HALLAM: Matthews. (*He spells it.*)

SELINCOURT: I've come to advise you not to be alarmed.

HALLAM: Extremely civil of you.

SELINCOURT: The conflict you will hear and see in a few minutes is merely an exercise, a mock battle, a prank of my own, designed to introduce my Local Defence Volunteers to the conditions they must expect in the forthcoming engagement with the Beast of the Apocalypse.

HALLAM: I beg your pardon?

SELINCOURT: The Fiend of the Bottomless Pit.

HALLAM: I still don't quite—

SELINCOURT: The Serpent of Corsica.

HALLAM: Oh, you mean—

SELINCOURT: Napoleon Bonaparte.

HALLAM: The heat – I think it must be the heat. Very hot today, is it not?

SELINCOURT: More than warm – more than warm.

HALLAM: Then that is undoubtedly the reason for my incapacity to make head or tail of anything that is said to me today. Your name, you say, is—

SELINCOURT: Selincourt. I am commander of the local forces – alas! so small – ranged against Bonaparte.

HALLAM: Yes, yes! I remember. I am with you. Continue.

SELINCOURT: It is my intention to begin a mock battle on, if I may put it so – (*Giggles*) – your doorstep. The noise may be considerable, not to say alarming. I have walked up to advise you of this. Would you be so kind as to warn Sir Timothy and other members of this household?

HALLAM: Delighted.

SELINCOURT: Thank you. Well, well! I must be off to see to the final disposal of my forces. Are you concerned with military matters, sir? But, of course, you must be.

HALLAM: Why?

SELINCOURT: Everyone must be in this hour of England's peril. Rather interesting: I have retained one-third of my forces under my command. The remaining two-thirds I am using as the enemy – a larger proportion, you notice, as will be the case. This 'enemy' will land from the sea – we

have commandeered the local fishing fleet for the occasion –
and I shall repulse them. Care to come along and watch?

HALLAM: No, thank you.

SELINCOURT: Ah! Conserving your energy for the real
thing, eh?

HALLAM: Yes.

SELINCOURT: What will be your precise duties when the
great moment comes? Have you any special qualifications?

HALLAM: I can run very fast.

SELINCOURT (*delighted*): Can you really? Then you may be
the very man I'm looking for. My word, this is lucky!

HALLAM: In what way?

SELINCOURT: Well, as a commander of the local forces it is
one of my responsibilities to arrange that at the moment of
invasion someone runs through the countryside putting up,
at certain points, a poster bearing information. This must
be done quickly and efficiently. Perhaps, for the sake of
your country, you would care to take on the job. I have a
specimen poster here. (*He takes out the poster which he
proceeds to unfold. It bears the single word, in large staring type,*
INVASION.) The price is twopence each, one and eight
the dozen, or one hundred for twelve shillings.

HALLAM: Am I expected to pay for them?

SELINCOURT: That's very good of you. Then I should
advise you to purchase them by the hundred. The simplest
arithmetic will show that you save four and eightpence on
each hundred bought. No need to make up your mind
immediately. Think it over. I'll leave this with you so that
you can keep it in mind. (*He pins the poster on the alcove beside*
HALLAM.) I've also borrowed a balloon from the local fair
to give a further touch of reality to the proceedings. That
goes up in half-an-hour. Now I really must be off. Goodbye.

HALLAM: Goodbye.

SELINCOURT *goes as* DORCAS *and* EDWARD *come into the
garden*.

EDWARD: That's what social reform is, nothing more—

DORCAS: But it's so simple! Why doesn't everybody do it at once?

They come farther into the garden, not seeing HALLAM *reclining in the alcove.*

DORCAS: Tell me that bit again. The Tom Paine. I want to hear it again.

EDWARD: 'When it shall be said in any country in the world my poor are happy; neither ignorance nor distress is to be found among them; my jails are empty of prisoners, my streets of beggars; the aged are not in want; the taxes are not oppressive; the rational world is my friend, because I am the friend of its happiness: When these things can be said, then may that country boast its Constitution and its Government.'

DORCAS: That's beautiful. It's like poetry.

EDWARD: You've got tears in your eyes.

DORCAS: I don't care. I think you are a most wonderful man.

EDWARD: Sweetheart, I didn't write it.

DORCAS: But you said it. (*Pause.*) Will you go on to London?

EDWARD: Yes, quite soon.

DORCAS: Shall I tell you something? Yes, I will. When we first met you thought I was a silly girl. Yes, you did. You *are* a silly girl, you said. And do you know what happened?

EDWARD: What?

DORCAS: I fell in love. (*Pause.*) It's quite all right. I don't expect any answer.

EDWARD: Then I won't say anything.

DORCAS: No, don't. Just for a minute, anyway. I've spent years wondering how I'd fall in love for the first time. It's very important to a woman, you know. I'll let you into a secret. I always thought it would ruin my life. There have been a number of times when I've died for love before I'd even started to live. In my head, of course. No, don't stop me. I've almost finished. After all, I'm still young enough to

talk about a very common experience as if it were the most
original thing in the world.

EDWARD: Go on.

DORCAS: I shall now say something very funny. Something
that you, and everybody else here, would flatly contradict.
Being in love seems to make life very simple. There, you
made a face. Don't pretend you didn't. I saw. Go on, be a
liberal, and let me enjoy my idiocy. Pooh, nobody understands how awful it is to be a child. All that loneliness and
muddle. All that anger. Well, it's over now. Thank you
very much. (*She lies back, looking at the sky.*) Do they look
as though they're about to fall?

EDWARD: What?

DORCAS: The heavens. That's what they're always telling us.
That's what your kind are always telling us. War, revolution, famine, some horror, is going to bring them down.
I think they'll stay up there. And so do you. Go on, admit it,
you really think they'll stay there, don't you?

EDWARD (*looks up; laughs*): Probably.

DORCAS (*after a moment*): You've never laughed before. Do it
again.

EDWARD: Make me.

DORCAS: Don't go to London.

EDWARD: I must.

DORCAS: All right, go, then. But don't become one of those
men for whom the idea of people gets to be more important than people themselves.

EDWARD: How old are you?

DORCAS: Seventeen.

EDWARD: Just for the moment I wondered.

DORCAS: Does it matter? Go. Go now.

EDWARD: What's this? A quarrel?

DORCAS: Yes, it is. Goodbye. (*She stares into the distance.*)

EDWARD: Goodbye.

   Neither of them move: silence.

DORCAS: Forgive me.

EDWARD: All forgotten.

Very faintly there is a bugle call from the beaches.

HESTER *comes from the house.*

HESTER: Ah, Dorcas. I never seem to be able to find you. What have you been doing?

DORCAS: Putting off childish ways.

HESTER: I see. (*To* EDWARD.) We lose our children, you know. They wander from us. There comes a day – this one, for example, and a very nice day it is, too – and a daughter, very much loved, whom one has got used to having about the place, sometimes a nuisance, more often a blessing, disappears. Nowhere to be found.

DORCAS: I'm here, Mama.

HESTER: Oh, you're there, yes. But where is small Dorcas? Where is she? Is it sad?

EDWARD: No.

HESTER: You're quite right, Mr—

EDWARD: Sterne.

HESTER: Mr Sterne, you're quite right. It's not at all sad.

DORCAS: I've something to tell you, Mama.

HESTER: And I've something to tell you. Is your news important?

DORCAS: Yes.

HESTER: So is mine. Now listen carefully. I have just heard from Lady Jerningham. She wants me to go and join the Amazon Corps she is forming in East Anglia. I am to command a platoon. This means that—

LAMPRETT *and the small* BOY *have wandered in from the orchard.*

HESTER: Ah, Lamprett—

LAMPRETT: My dear?

HESTER: I am telling Dorcas—

TIMOTHY *comes from the house.*

– that I have heard from Lady Jerningham.

LAMPRETT: Such a pleasant woman.

HESTER: She wishes me to go up to East Anglia to command a platoon in what she calls her Amazon Corps. It is being formed so that the women of England may exercise their natural power of command. I am to be a Sergeant-Major. Stand up straight, Lamprett.

LAMPRETT: Sorry, my dear.

HESTER: I shall be leaving almost immediately, this evening at the latest. I understand that there are recruits to be disciplined. Dorcas will look after the house in my absence. You understand, Dorcas?

DORCAS: Yes, Mama.

TIMOTHY: Are you going to wear uniform?

HESTER: Certainly.

TIMOTHY: Breeches, I suppose! Eh, Lamprett. (*He is seized by quite immoderate laughter.*)

HESTER: I understand that Lady Jerningham has designed the undress uniform herself. An undergarment in the shade of *fumée de Londres* with a cloak and cap of *grisantique*. In action, of course, we shall wear something very different.

LAMPRETT: And I'm sure you'll look very handsome.

BREEZE *comes in from the orchard.*

TIMOTHY: I wish something would happen. It distresses me to see everyone standing about like this when we might be getting on with the job of throwing the French into the sea.

LAMPRETT *is examining the poster bearing the stark word* INVASION.

What's that? Another cattle sale?

LAMPRETT: No.

TIMOTHY *comes to beside* LAMPRETT *and sees the wording of the poster.*

TIMOTHY: Lamprett! (*He turns from the poster: then, spinning round, again transfixes it.*) It remains! Lamprett, can I believe my eyes?

LAMPRETT: You can.

TIMOTHY: But that's it, man!

LAMPRETT: Yes.

TIMOTHY: What I've been waiting for.

LAMPRETT: Yes.

TIMOTHY: The official instructions – I remember them well. Part Four, Section VIII: At the landing of enemy troops runners will pass through the countryside liberally distributing bills bearing the single word, INVASION. These bills may be purchased, price twopence each – (*He breaks off, removing his hat.*) Ladies and gentlemen, it is upon us. Like a thief in the night in broad daylight it is upon us.

All stand in a reverent silence. Distantly from the direction of the coast, a bugle sounds a military call. TIMOTHY *at the top of his voice shouts*:

Humpage!

HUMPAGE (*awakes*): Sir!

TIMOTHY: Anything to report? Was that man asleep, can anyone tell me? Was he? Anything to report, Humpage?

HUMPAGE: Yes, sir.

TIMOTHY: Something in sight?

HUMPAGE: Yes, sir.

TIMOTHY: Something suspicious?

HUMPAGE: Oh, yes, sir!

TIMOTHY: Ships of war?

HUMPAGE: Oh, yes, yes, sir!

TIMOTHY: Troops?

HUMPAGE: Oh, sir – oh, sir – yes, yes, yes, sir! One, two, three, four, five—

He continues to count aloud in a growing agony and panic as the scene proceeds.

TIMOTHY: Every man for himself!

LAMPRETT: What's that?

TIMOTHY: Every man for himself! (*He rushes into the house.*)

HUMPAGE:–thirty-seven, thirty-eight, thirty-nine, forty. Oh, God! Forty, forty-one, forty-two—

The action within the garden becomes confused. From the general activity the following can be heard.

LAMPRETT: Humpage!

HUMPAGE: – fifty-seven, fifty-eight – yes, sir? – fifty-nine, sixty—

LAMPRETT: You must on no account allow this diversion to distract you from your primary duty.

HUMPAGE: No, sir – sixty-five, sixty-six, sixty-seven—

LAMPRETT: Fires, Humpage, fires!

HUMPAGE: Yes, sir. Seventy, seventy-one—

> BREEZE *speaks to* HUMPAGE.

BREEZE: You want to be careful up there, you know.

LAMPRETT: Don't distract him, if you please.

BREEZE: Sorry, sir.

LAMPRETT: No point in alarming him. We must all take our chance. What are you going to do?

BREEZE: I shall have to look after Mr Matthews.

LAMPRETT: Well, if you'll take my advice—

> HESTER *is speaking to the small* BOY.

HESTER: Well, it looks as if we're going to have to stand and fight. Try and choose someone your own size. There's no point being quixotic in war. Be an Englishman. Stand alongside me. And what are you laughing at?

> DORCAS *is speaking to* EDWARD.

DORCAS: You know about this sort of thing. What does one do?

EDWARD: Don't stand under a flag, stay far away from anybody in a fine bright uniform, take a look at the sun so that you'll always know which way you're running, if there's a loaf of bread about put it in your pocket, and if there's a hole in the ground sit in it. Ignore all cries for help, stay deaf to all exhortations, and keep your trousers tied tight about your waist. In any difficulty, look stupid, and at the first opportunity go to sleep.

DORCAS: But that's the philosophy of a coward!

EDWARD: Nonsense. It's the philosophy of a common soldier. Men have conquered the world with it.

HESTER: Lamprett, what are your intentions?

LAMPRETT: What's that, my dear?

HESTER: Your intentions. What are they in this emergency?

LAMPRETT: To stand by, my dear, until required.

HESTER: And when will that be?

LAMPRETT: It will be when the first spark, flash, flame, scintillation, blaze or conflagration is reported. And then—

BREEZE: Excuse me, sir.

LAMPRETT: What is it?

BREEZE: Do you think it would be wise to wake Mr Matthews now?

LAMPRETT: Wake him?

BREEZE: He's sleeping at the moment and he does so dislike being woken. Could you again advise me, Mr Bellboys? Does the emergency warrant so grave a liberty?

LAMPRETT: As waking him? I should say so. Wouldn't you, my dear?

HESTER: Yes, Breeze. I think you may wake him.

BREEZE: Thank you, ma'am.

He crosses to HALLAM *and stands looking down at him.*

HESTER: This will make it necessary for me to expedite my departure, Lamprett. At any moment you may be seeing the last of me.

LAMPRETT: I hope not, my dear.

HESTER: Temporarily, I mean.

LAMPRETT: I must have a word with Hallam.

He goes to HALLAM, *who, gently shaken by* BREEZE, *is coming to consciousness.*

BREEZE: Excuse me, sir. The invasion.

HALLAM: Thank you, Sam. (*He discovers* LAMPRETT *standing over him.*)

LAMPRETT: Hallam!

HALLAM: My dear fellow?

LAMPRETT (*he holds out his hand*): Goodbye.

HALLAM: You're off?

LAMPRETT: Certainly not! I'm standing by.

HALLAM: Then why—?

LAMPRETT: The situation is grave.

HALLAM: Yes, yes! Goodbye.

LAMPRETT: The lieutenant of my brigade was burnt to a cinder two months ago in what was merely a civil conflagration. Don't tell the women.

HALLAM: About your lieutenant?

LAMPRETT: No, no. About the danger to me at the moment.

HALLAM: Of course. Not a word, I assure you.

LAMPRETT: Thank you.

    They shake hands. LAMPRETT *then salutes and marches away with the small* BOY.

HUMPAGE: One hundred and fourteen – one hundred and fifteen!

HALLAM: What's that fellow doing?

BREEZE: Counting the enemy forces, I imagine.

HALLAM: Oh, dear!

BREEZE: Would you like to retire to a place of safety, sir?

HALLAM: I don't think so. I'm very comfortable here.

HESTER: What are you children going to do?

DORCAS: What do you suggest, Mama?

HESTER: I really don't know.

DORCAS: In that case we'll just sit here and wait for something to happen.

    It does – in a tremendous cannonade from the beaches and, simultaneously, the appearance of TIMOTHY *in the doorway of the house. He is dressed for his impersonation of Bonaparte: the resemblance is very startling. Firmly grasped in his right hand is the French phrase book.*

TIMOTHY: *Halte-là! Où est mon baton? Il n'est pas dans mon havresac!* (*He roars with laughter.*) Good, eh? I'm really pleased. But no nonsense! Humpage!

HUMPAGE: One hundred and sixteen.

TIMOTHY: One hundred and sixteen what?

HUMPAGE: Men, sir.

TIMOTHY: Nonsense! There are one hundred and seventy-five thousand men. You can't count anyway – you know that.

Again there is a bugle call from the beaches – followed this time by the rattle of musketry.

TIMOTHY: Obviously no time to be lost. They are ashore. Humpage!

HUMPAGE: Sir!

TIMOTHY: You may ring the bell and put up the signals. I am ready.

HUMPAGE: Thank you, sir.

He is galvanized into action. The clangour of the great brass bell rings out. The signal flaps whirl and wave, finally coming to rest to show an ominous scarlet. LAMPRETT, in uniform, rushes in with the BOY.

LAMPRETT: No! Humpage! No! You'll call out the brigade! Ah! Damn the invasion.

HESTER: Lamprett!

LAMPRETT: Well, my dear, what shall I say to the men when they arrive?

TIMOTHY: If your men have any spirit they'll already be on the beaches fighting the French, and not waiting for you to show them some miserable little fire they can fight.

LAMPRETT: Oh, what a thing to say! My men are brave and good and true. Bless them! (*Then – very maliciously, he says:*) And if you, Timothy, think that by dressing yourself up as Lord Nelson—

TIMOTHY (*furious*): Lord Nelson!

LAMPRETT: – and running away – if you think by that you are helping your country, then I'm a Dutchman.

TIMOTHY: You're a damned ignorant fool, I know that. Anyway, I've no time for a row with you. Hallam!

LAMPRETT: Well, don't say horrid things about my brigade, then.

    He moves to HESTER, *who consoles him.*

TIMOTHY: Hallam!

HALLAM: Timothy?

TIMOTHY: You recall your promise?

HALLAM: My—

TIMOTHY (*he points to the well*): The initial part of the plan.

HALLAM: Yes, indeed.

TIMOTHY: I am quite ready. If you will take the handle, I will grasp the rope and stand in the bucket. On the command from me – lower!

    HALLAM *has moved to the well and now miserably takes hold of the handle.*

Got it?

    HALLAM *nods.*

Right!

    TIMOTHY *puts both feet into the bucket and takes hold of the rope.* HALLAM *takes the strain of his weight.*

Am I clear?

HALLAM: I think so.

TIMOTHY: A last word to everyone. Should I not return there must be no tears. I go on this mission of my own free will, giving my services—

HALLAM: Timothy!

TIMOTHY: – to my country with a good heart. Those that have gone before me and those that will come after me—

HALLAM: Timothy!

TIMOTHY: What is it, Hallam!

HALLAM (*breathlessly*): Last words should be spoken before entering the bucket.

TIMOTHY: What? Oh, sorry! Well – (*He consults the phrase book.*) *Au revoir, mes amis, au revoir. Là! Descendons maintenant.*

HALLAM *begins to lower.* TIMOTHY *and the bucket remain unmoving, the rope wreathing itself about* TIMOTHY.

Can you release me? I seem to be caught in something. (*In his little struggle,* TIMOTHY *glances at the sky. He is immediately transfixed.*) What's that?

Everyone looks up: they are lost in wonder

HUMPAGE: It's a balloon!

HESTER: Bless me! What a pretty thing!

DORCAS: Edward – an air-balloon – above us.

HUMPAGE: You'd never get me into one of them.

TIMOTHY: That's an idea. I like that. (*He catches sight of* LAMPRETT: *he remembers.*) Lord Nelson!

Suddenly he descends the well. There is a loud cry from everyone – followed by an explosion.

CURTAIN

.

NOTE: During the interval martial music of an heroic nature should be played – together with distant trumpet calls and drum rolls – bursts of cheering and perhaps an explosion.

ACT TWO

The scene is the same.

The time: later the same day.

The battle may have passed this way for there are sounds of military activity from a little way off. A drum rolls ominously and a voice shouts commands at intervals. Across the garden drifts a cloud of smoke and from an upper part of the house flies a tattered banner – a symbol of resistance, it can only be supposed.

HUMPAGE *remains at his post.*

The garden is otherwise empty, but the fire-engine has been brought in. This stands at the ready, pulsating with the need for action. From the engine a length of hose runs out of the garden below the house.

After a moment LAMPRETT *appears rolling in the hose which he stores away on the engine. He adjusts a complication of valves: the engine becomes silent and still, and some kind of order is restored.* LAMPRETT *sits on the engine and looks hopefully at* HUMPAGE, *who shakes his head.*

LAMPRETT: Then we can but wait. For I'll not believe that this day – so-called Armageddon – can pass without our being needed.

The small BOY *comes into the garden.* LAMPRETT *speaks to him.*

Nothing yet, I'm afraid.

The BOY *sits beside* LAMPRETT.

Could you grasp that lever there? Thank you. It controls something. I have to look after it like a child, you know. For example, the cold atmosphere makes the thing fret in a quite distressing manner. But today is very warm. (*He pauses.*) Ironic, isn't it, that the only place we have a fire is inside the engine. But I've long ceased to believe in the art of reasoning. When I was a young man at the university I studied logic and it led to dreadful conclusions. Such fearful results came from attempting to arrange my thoughts. No, I cannot tell you! However, on some subjects my mind is clear.

The MAIDSERVANT *has come into the garden from the house carrying the necessities for a picnic meal, which she proceeds to lay out on the ground.*

I'm an example of the man of learning turned man of action by necessity. Yet, I will confess, there are times when I'm tempted to retire, put up my feet, draw my cap over my eyes and let the world burn away around me.

HESTER *comes from the house.*

HESTER: Pippin!

MAID: Yes, ma'am?

HESTER: As much food as possible, I think. We cannot tell how many we shall be called upon to feed and succour on a day like this.

MAID: Very good, ma'am.

HESTER: I thought, Lamprett, we'd eat out here. A fine, if rather noisy day. I don't want people tramping all over the house, you know.

LAMPRETT: Quite right.

HESTER: We should have eaten before this but the household arrangements are a little upset. Forgive me.

LAMPRETT: More than understandable in the circumstances.

She is looking at the fire-engine.

Is the engine in your way?

HESTER: Well, perhaps—

LAMPRETT: Yes, I can see you wish me to move it.

HESTER: We are all aware of its usefulness. But at mealtimes, do you think—

LAMPRETT: Very well.

LAMPRETT *and the* BOY *move the engine from the garden.*

HESTER: Pippin, run into the house. You'll find some wine in the cooler. Bring it to me.

The MAID *goes into the house.* HESTER *sits on the ground beside the picnic meal.*

There is great comfort, I find, in resorting to good food during a crisis. Man's behaviour to man would be less ungenerous if everyone ate regular meals. For when conversation fails, how much better to resort to the knife and fork than to the sword and trumpet.

HUMPAGE: Are you speaking to me?

HESTER: Not necessarily.

LAMPRETT *returns with the* BOY.

HESTER: Come along. Everything is ready.

LAMPRETT: How charming! It would appear it takes a siege to return us to the pleasures of our youth.

HESTER: Indeed, it must be thirty years, Lamprett, since you and I sat together in the sun.

LAMPRETT: There has been much to do in that time. Come, little boy, don't be shy.

HESTER: Join us, please.

The BOY *joins them at the meal. The* MAID *comes from the house, carrying the wine.*

LAMPRETT: Ah! You anticipate my wishes. A glass of wine to rinse from me the staleness of approaching age. Have some, little boy—

HESTER: With water!

LAMPRETT: – but always remember – 'Drink not the third glass – which thou canst not tame when once it is within thee!'

They laugh gently at the child. The MAID *returns to the house.*

HESTER: Tell me, Lamprett, is it reprehensible that we should enjoy a moment's peace?

LAMPRETT: I should say not, my dear. Let us enjoy it whilst

we can. You may be assured we shall be brought to rude fact at any moment by some disgraceful incident.

HESTER: Which reminds me to ask you something. But first – I'll just take the merrythought from the chicken.

LAMPRETT: These bouches are delicious. What was it you wished to ask?

HESTER: Concerning rude fact, I fear.

LAMPRETT: Never mind. We must face it.

HUMPAGE: Excuse me.

HESTER: What was at the bottom of the well?

HUMPAGE: Excuse me.

LAMPRETT: What is it? (*To* HESTER.) Harsh reality, alas, is ever with us.

HUMPAGE: Might I have some form of protection?

LAMPRETT: Protection against what?

HUMPAGE: Missiles, I think they're called.

LAMPRETT: Are you being shot at? At this very moment – are you being shot at?

HUMPAGE: No, sir.

LAMPRETT: But you think it may happen soon?

HUMPAGE: Yes, sir. And I fear for my life.

LAMPRETT *takes a dish from among the picnic, empties it, and carries it to* HUMPAGE.

LAMPRETT: Try wearing this. It will afford you some kind of protection.

HUMPAGE: Yes, sir.

LAMPRETT: You cannot expect both to look handsome and be safe, can you?

HUMPAGE: No, sir.

LAMPRETT: Is it comfortable?

HUMPAGE: No, sir.

LAMPRETT: But you think it will do?

HUMPAGE: Yes, sir.

LAMPRETT: Good. (*An afterthought.*) It doesn't obscure your vision, does it?

HUMPAGE: No, sir.

LAMPRETT (*a second afterthought*): It is a saucepan, you know.

HUMPAGE: Yes, sir. (*He adjusts the headgear.*)

LAMPRETT: Must look after the servants in this business. Quite incapable of doing so themselves. You were saying, my dear – before that absurd interruption by Humpage complaining of the danger of his somewhat exposed position? (*He glances at* HUMPAGE *who is immediately suffused by shame.*) You were saying—

HESTER: I asked – what was at the bottom of the well?

LAMPRETT: Darkness and dirt, and a most peculiar, rather interesting smell.

HESTER: No water?

LAMPRETT: Oh, dear no!

HESTER: And, as you said, no Timothy.

LAMPRETT: Not a sign of him.

HESTER: May I say, Lamprett, that I consider you showed the most admirable courage in volunteering to descend the well in search of Timothy.

LAMPRETT: Well, after all, he is my brother. And it provided an excuse for doing something I've always wanted to do.

HESTER: Descend the well?

LAMPRETT: Yes. Now I have, so to speak, broken the ice I may make it a regular habit.

HESTER: Have you any idea what Timothy is about?

LAMPRETT: No idea at all.

HESTER: What was the purpose of the uniform he was wearing?

LAMPRETT: Ah, that! Foolish of me to mistake it for an impersonation of Lord Nelson – it was obviously the uniform of the Consular Service. From that we can draw but one conclusion.

HESTER: Which is—?

LAMPRETT: That he is attempting to escape the country.

There is a loud explosion a little way off.

HESTER: Do you think we shall ever see him again?

LAMPRETT: I very much doubt that. It would appear that he was successful in getting away. I shall, of course, take over the administration of the estate from today and—

Through the open orchard gate there rolls, very slowly, a cannon-ball. It traverses the garden and comes to rest at LAMPRETT's *feet.*

– I may say that under my direction—

HESTER: What is that?

LAMPRETT: A cannon-ball, my dear. Under my direction things here will be very different. I've never agreed to the subordination of certain public services, such as the fire brigade, to ephemeral activities such as agriculture. My views—

There is a loud explosion.

– will now be put into practice and I think we can look forward—

Through the open gate a second cannon-ball comes fairly bounding into the garden. It comes to rest by the first.

– to an era which will be without parallel—

HESTER: Lamprett!

LAMPRETT: My dear?

HESTER: Shut the gate.

He does so, saying:

LAMPRETT: – an era without parallel in the history of the county.

HESTER: Where is everyone?

LAMPRETT: Whom do you mean by everyone?

HESTER: Well, Dorcas and her young man. And Hallam – Hallam Matthews, where is he?

LAMPRETT: The last I saw of him was when he was being led away by his servant after his regrettable behaviour with Timothy and the well. I've no idea where they were making for.

HALLAM *and* BREEZE *come into the garden from the orchard.*

But wherever it was, they are returned.

HALLAM: Hester. Lamprett.

HESTER: How are you, Hallam?

HALLAM: Shaken, but recovering.

HESTER: I'm pleased to hear that.

HALLAM: What is happening?

LAMPRETT: At the moment? Well, the battle – if it can be called such – appears to have moved somewhat to the west. With regard to the general situation it is fluid. Anything may happen.

HALLAM: Oh, dear!

LAMPRETT: Don't fret, my dear fellow. I am now in charge.

HALLAM: Any sign of Timothy?

LAMPRETT: None. Apparently he was successful in his escape.

HALLAM: Escape! No, no, my dear Lamprett, you have misunderstood his intentions.

LAMPRETT: I think not—

HALLAM: But I can assure you—

LAMPRETT: No more, if you please! The subject is delicate. What I do not understand is this: an invasion in force but no fires. Not one. I cannot believe that Bonaparte and his Generals can have underestimated the effect upon a civil population of a good wholesome blaze. But that is apparently the case. Not a fire within sight. (*Shouting.*) Is there, Humpage?

HUMPAGE: No, sir.

LAMPRETT: Although how you should know with that pot crammed over your eyes in that preposterous fashion is beyond me!

    HUMPAGE *prises the saucepan from his forehead.*

Better! Anything to report?

HUMPAGE: No, sir.

LAMPRETT (*to* HALLAM): You see?

HALLAM: I admit that things seem unnaturally quiet.

LAMPRETT: The lull, perhaps, before the storm.

HALLAM: Please don't say that!

DORCAS and EDWARD come in from the orchard.

DORCAS: Ah, Mama! Have you recovered Uncle Timothy yet?

HESTER: Don't be frivolous, my dear.

DORCAS: *Là! Descendons maintenant!* Bump! (*She laughs.*)

HALLAM: Heartless child.

DORCAS: Do the present remarkable and unforeseen circumstances upset your plans, dear Mama?

LAMPRETT: What's the child saying?

DORCAS: A simple question, Papa. Does the loss of Uncle Timothy prevent Mama from taking up her duties as Sergeant-Major to the Amazons of Norfolk? Or do we all, in that very English way, refuse to admit that 'Something has happened' and proceed to carry on as if nothing ever could – happen, I mean – that we didn't ourselves intend?

HESTER: Whatever is the matter with you, Dorcas?

DORCAS: I'm happy, Mama.

HESTER: That's no excuse for talking the most utter nonsense.

DORCAS: Yes, it is. I'm in love.

LAMPRETT: This is no time to be falling in love, Dorcas. At any other time – yes, yes! – your mother and I would be only too pleased, but now there is much to be done. (*He speaks to the BOY.*) Come with me, little boy.

DORCAS: Where are you taking him?

LAMPRETT: I'm instructing him in the rudimentary principles of fire-fighting. He knows nothing about it. Quite ignorant. It is ridiculous, this business of not letting children play with fire when they are babies.

He goes out with the BOY.

HESTER: Hallam, I'm wondering if I might borrow your servant, Breeze, for a short while.

HALLAM: Most certainly, my dear Hester, but take care not to damage him.

HESTER: The reason is this: among the accoutrements Lady Jerningham has sent to me is a large brass breastplate. This is in a quite shockingly dilapidated condition. It occurred to me that Breeze might be the very person to refurbish it.

BREEZE: Certainly, ma'am.

HALLAM: That's right, Sam. Go with Mrs Bellboys and do your best. What is your experience with breastplates?

BREEZE: Very limited, sir.

HALLAM: Never mind. Do all you can.

HESTER: None of us can do more.

BREEZE *follows* HESTER *into the house.*

HALLAM: I am contemplating the effect on my digestion of eating during a battle.

He fusses over the little meal before him: DORCAS *and* EDWARD *regard him with kindness.*

DORCAS: Mr Matthews—

HALLAM: Yes?

DORCAS: Are you really so deeply concerned about yourself?

HALLAM: Certainly.

DORCAS: You mean you don't have to pretend?

HALLAM: Not any more.

DORCAS: Did you once?

HALLAM: Oh, yes. When I was about – (*He nods at* EDWARD) – his age.

DORCAS: Now wars can break out, monsters can land in the country, the marvels of science and art can threaten us all with destruction, but none of it matters so long as Hallam Matthews gets through luncheon without indigestion.

HALLAM: You've obviously never had indigestion. What are you asking me to do? Put up a defence?

DORCAS: I think you should.

HALLAM: Well, first of all find me a napkin, or cloth, or something of the sort.

DORCAS *does so.*

The conservatism of middle-age worries you, doesn't it?

You don't seem to understand that if I'd stayed as vulnerable as I was when I was a young man I'd never have survived. All right, Mr Sterne, it might have been a good thing if I hadn't. You'll forgive me if I believe otherwise.

EDWARD: Of course.

HALLAM: I'll tell you something. I sat in this garden fourteen years ago. It was a day very much like this. I had come down from London because I had fallen in love. I was so shaken by the intensity of my feeling that I had to put some distance between myself and the girl to understand what was happening to me. I sat here and wrote poetry. I babbled on to your mother and father about my passion. The words I both wrote and spoke came from my heart, and at the time were sincere, and not without beauty. Yet if they could be heard again in this garden we'd all be blushing. That is why old songs and dead fashion, which can make me cry, only make you laugh. That's what time can do. Cover my face.

DORCAS *goes to* HALLAM, *and kisses him.*

Thank you, Dorcas. They talk about the folly of youth. Keep your folly, Mr Sterne, but also pray that you grow into as handsome and nice old gentleman as I'm going to be.

DORCAS: What happened to the girl?

HALLAM: She married. Where's the war?

DORCAS: Gone away for the moment.

HALLAM: I feel much better. How are you going to change the world, Mr Sterne?

EDWARD: By conviction.

HALLAM: And who are you going to convince?

EDWARD: Everybody.

HALLAM: Starting where? Top or bottom? That's something which has always confused me about reform. Where to begin.

EDWARD: Start with the people.

HALLAM (*doubtfully*): Yes. But they're always a little slow to follow on.

EDWARD: All right, then. Start at the top, with the heads of state.

HALLAM: My dear boy, do you know what you're saying? Here we are on the brink of war, and the head of the state is a dear, silly man. At the moment we call him eccentric. In a few years we shall be forced to call him something else.

EDWARD: Well, there's your hereditary monarchy for you.

HALLAM: And what has your democracy thrown up on the other side? This frightful little Bonaparte person, who's just had himself crowned with considerably more splendour than Westminster Abbey has ever seen. He has that awful wife, and the bottoms of his family cover almost every throne in Europe. No, no, my dear Sterne, men of good will, such as ourselves, will have to find a third course.

EDWARD: If you're suggesting what I think you're suggesting the answer is – never!

HALLAM: I was afraid you'd say that. No compromise, eh?

EDWARD: Radicalism has a purity, Matthews, which is probably beyond your comprehension.

HALLAM: All right, my dear fellow, keep your political virginity, but don't be upset if others get on with governing the world. Let's not quarrel.

DORCAS: No. I won't allow it.

HALLAM: Take her away, Sterne. She'll never be my sweetheart, but give me another half-hour with her and she'd be voting for me, if she could, in an election. She's a woman, you see. Off you go.

  EDWARD *and* DORCAS *move across the garden. They go.*
  The small BOY *has come into the garden. He and* HALLAM *look at each other doubtfully.* HALLAM *speaks:*

HALLAM: Are you going to attack me? I suppose that's what my kind exists for. Very well, get it over. No? Then let's sit down.

  HALLAM *holds out his hand to the* BOY, *who takes it. They walk together to the alcove, and sit.*

Lovely day. Yes. (*A pause.*) You must learn to talk about the weather. (*A pause.*) Very boring, this war, don't you think? I came down here to get away from it, you know. But it's with us, like other things one would like to escape from. Love, for example. I don't suppose it bothers you at the moment. But there's your friend in front of my eyes: I'm reminded of the past. They're happy, those two. What are you? What am I? Never mind, we must cheer up. As has been said, *On n'est jamais si heureux ni si malheureux qu'on s'imagine.*

The small BOY *finds this very funny indeed.* HALLAM *stares at him.*

I can't make you laugh, but de la Rochefoucauld can.

There is a bugle call from not far off.

And there's all this talk about the equality of man. That worries me very much. What ground do you and I meet on? It's a problem, isn't it? Forty years must separate us. We know nothing about each other, and seem quite incapable of telling. (*A pause.*) Those eyes of yours have seen more than they should. I don't know why I feel that, but somehow I understand why you reject the weather, the war and other trivial matters, such as love and justice, as subjects for conversation.

GEORGE SELINCOURT, *accompanied by three of his fencibles – the* REVEREND JOSEPH BROTHERHOOD, JAMES GIDDY *and* RUFUS PIGGOTT – *marches into the garden. They are, each of them, in a state of considerable alarm and confusion. Each is armed to a certain degree: there is not an element of uniformity about their clothes.* GEORGE SELINCOURT *shepherds them forward, crying out.*

SELINCOURT: Now, please, gentlemen, please! Sort yourselves out! The first principle of modern warfare is to accept an unexpected occurrence with equity, dignity and discipline. Discipline, Piggott!

PIGGOTT *is greeting* HUMPAGE *with enthusiasm.*

And we do not consort with members of other units. Now, then.

The tiny Corps is lined up and now stands to attention.

Oh, good! Very, very good! (SELINCOURT, *for only a moment, is lost in admiration.*) Your hat, Reverend Sir – (*He speaks to* BROTHERHOOD) – perhaps just a trifle forward.

BROTHERHOOD *adjusts his hat.*

Excellent! Excellent! Now, gentlemen, the situation which has arisen has quite confounded my original plans for today. I have therefore rearranged my notions with speed and skill. The mark of the modern soldier, gentlemen. Giddy!

GIDDY: Sir!

SELINCOURT: You will mount guard over this gate.

GIDDY *falls out to take up his place.*

Piggott!

PIGGOTT: What?

SELINCOURT: You will mount guard on some object over there.

PIGGOTT *falls out to take his place.*

SELINCOURT: And you, Reverend Sir, will be so kind as to keep an eye on the front door of this house.

BROTHERHOOD *takes up his position.*

This, gentlemen, is to prevent any possible attack on my rear. Ever vulnerable, according to the text books. (*He regards his men.*) Excellent – excellent!

HALLAM *and the* BOY *have sat watching these manœuvres.*

HALLAM (*to the* BOY): Military matters make for such a gross invasion of privacy, don't they?

SELINCOURT *discovers* HALLAM *and the* BOY.

SELINCOURT: Excuse me—

HALLAM: Yes?

SELINCOURT: You are the gentleman I saw earlier today.

HALLAM: Am I?

SELINCOURT: You are.

HALLAM: You must forgive me but I cannot recall ever having seen you in my life before.

SELINCOURT: Come, come! Only a little time ago I saw you.

HALLAM: You did, sir?

SELINCOURT: And now I want to see you again.

HALLAM: And so you shall.

SELINCOURT: First, I must ask you not to be afraid of, or intimidated by, my fencibles.

HALLAM: Certainly not. You may rest assured on that point. (*A pause.*) Where are they?

SELINCOURT *indicates* BROTHERHOOD, GIDDY *and* PIGGOTT. HALLAM *peers from the alcove.*

HALLAM: Ah, yes. Fencibles, eh? Is that all you have?

SELINCOURT: No, indeed not! There are ninety-six at the ready on the beaches and cliffs, every one alert, crafty and massively courageous. The gentlemen you see here are my personal bodyguard. Mr Matthews—

HALLAM: That is my name.

SELINCOURT: Mr Matthews, at our previous meeting today I grievously misled you.

HALLAM: I'm very sorry to hear that.

SELINCOURT: Through no fault of my own, may I add?

HALLAM: No, no!

SELINCOURT: The fact is—

HALLAM: Yes?

SELINCOURT: Shall I come straight to the point?

HALLAM: Please do.

SELINCOURT: Time is short.

HALLAM: Yes, indeed.

SELINCOURT: Very well then. This that you hear—

Obligingly, in the distance, there is a roll of drums and a bugle call.

– this is no elementary exercise in tactics, no mere manoeuvre, but the Real Thing!

HALLAM: You mean—

SELINCOURT: I mean, sir, that Napoleon Bonaparte has landed in England! (*There is a suitable pause.*)

HALLAM: You've seen him?

SELINCOURT: No, not myself. But Mr Brotherhood, here, has seen him in circumstances which – but he might care to explain himself. He is the local Rector, you know. Mr Brotherhood!

BROTHERHOOD *comes forward.*

Tell your story again, Mr Brotherhood.

BROTHERHOOD *proceeds to do so in a commendably military manner.*

BROTHERHOOD: Sir: whilst sitting at a point of vantage on the cliff top and partaking of a small alfresco meal—

SELINCOURT: I provide my men with rations for the field.

HALLAM: Bravo!

SELINCOURT: At my own expense, of course. Proceed, Mr Brotherhood.

BROTHERHOOD: – an alfresco meal which I was interested to note was wrapped in some pages of George Herbert's poems, I was suddenly confronted by what, at first, I took to be an apparition. This fiend seemed to rise from the ground before my eyes. I was about to pronounce an exorcism when the creature shouted: *Me voici, Monsieur!* The combination of the French tongue and sudden recognition of the uniform worn gave me to understand that I was confronted by none other than the French Emperor, Bonaparte.

HALLAM (*fascinated*): What did you do?

BROTHERHOOD: I ran at once to my superior officer.

SELINCOURT: That's me. We returned to the place together and there was no sign of anyone. But – and I think this important – someone had stolen Mr Brotherhood's bag of biscuits.

HALLAM: Was Bonaparte alone when you saw him, Mr Brotherhood?

SELINCOURT: Ah! That is the confusing point. Bonaparte has landed here, but where are his men?

HALLAM: I can honestly disclaim that I'm concealing them.

SELINCOURT: A confusing point, but I have the solution.

HALLAM: Yes?

SELINCOURT: His men are under the sea.

HALLAM: Under the sea!

SELINCOURT: Yes. Bonaparte, intrepid fellow that he is – we must admit that – come, in fairness we must admit it – Bonaparte has come ashore to spy out the lie of the land. His armies wait for his signal and then when it is given they will pour from the tunnel in their thousands.

HALLAM: Tunnel, sir!

SELINCOURT: The tunnel beneath the sea, Mr Matthews. You must have read your newspapers. The method of Bonaparte's arrival has long been a matter for conjecture. Some – and I must admit myself to have once been of their number – some favoured the monster bridge to have been constructed by his engineers. A vast project thrown across the breadth of the Channel, and over which Bonaparte's armies would have marched in their thousands. You may return to your post, Reverend Sir.

BROTHERHOOD: Sir!

He goes back to the door of the house and takes up a defensive attitude.

SELINCOURT: Another school of thought – profoundly unimaginative – took it that he would transport his armies on a series of giant rafts. (*He whispers.*) Mr Brotherhood once confided to me that he was of the opinion that by some diabolical power the French would walk to England.

HALLAM: On the water?

SELINCOURT: Yes.

HALLAM: God bless my soul!

SELINCOURT: He's a very good man: he believes in the Devil. The last conjecture – which we can now substantiate as fact – was that Bonaparte would arrive through a vast tunnel bored beneath the sea. This he has done. His armies doubtless wait below for his signal. (*He looks at the ground with some satisfaction.*) Rather like standing on a volcano, isn't it?

HALLAM: Then all, I take it, is lost.

SELINCOURT: Certainly not!

HALLAM: What are you going to do?

BREEZE *has come into the garden from the house.*

BREEZE: Mr Matthews, sir.

HALLAM: Just a moment, Sam. (*To* SELINCOURT.) What are you going to do?

SELINCOURT: All that is necessary. I told you that the French armies await a signal from the Emperor.

HALLAM: Yes.

SELINCOURT: That signal will never be given. We shall prevent it. We shall catch him – oh, yes, by heaven! – the hunt is up and we shall catch him. Meantime I've given instructions for the signal fires to be lighted. There they are, burning well. One, two, three, four – and there goes another – and yet another.

LAMPRETT *runs into the garden. He is properly accoutred, wearing his helmet and carrying another in his hand. He sees the small* BOY *and, going to him, crams the second helmet on the wretched child's head before snatching him up. He then goes out at a run with the boy literally tucked beneath his arm.*

SELINCOURT *has observed this: he shakes his head.*

SELINCOURT: First sign of panic. (*He turns to* HALLAM.) As for your accepted duties, Mr Matthews, I have your materials here.

HALLAM: I beg your pardon?

SELINCOURT *has taken a large roll of invasion posters from* GIDDY.

SELINCOURT: You will remember – (*He unrolls a poster before* HALLAM.) – and my plea is: run, Mr Matthews, run!

Through every town, village and hamlet spread the news with feverish haste. Run, Mr Matthews, run till you drop! Twelve shillings.

HALLAM: What's that?

SELINCOURT: There are one hundred posters. At the authorized reduction, that is twelve shillings.

    HALLAM *produces a sovereign.*

I've no change.

HALLAM: Neither have I.

SELINCOURT: I'll owe it to you.

    He takes the sovereign, leaving HALLAM *clasping the bundle of posters.*

We must be off! Squad!

    The FENCIBLES *assemble in some kind of order.*

Off we go!

    And off they go except the REVEREND MR BROTHERHOOD, *who lags behind to ask:*

BROTHERHOOD: Are you Hallam Matthews author of *A Critical Inquiry into the Nature of Ecclesiastical Cant?*

HALLAM: 'With a Supplementary Dissertation on Lewd Lingo'. Yes, I am.

BROTHERHOOD: You should be ashamed! (*Then he, too, is gone.*)

BREEZE: Can I relieve you of those, sir?

HALLAM: What's that, Sam? Oh, yes, thank you very much. (*He gives the roll of posters to* BREEZE.)

BREEZE: Forgive me if I anticipate, sir, but do you wish me to run through the countryside with a feverish haste?

HALLAM: No, Sam. I don't want you to do anything of the kind.

BREEZE: I overheard your conversation with that gentleman, sir. I was just inside that door. I wasn't going to show myself, but I saw you were getting into difficulties.

HALLAM: God bless you, Sam.

BREEZE: I suppose it's Sir Timothy they've seen, sir, and

mistaken him, as is only natural in that get-up, for Boney.

HALLAM: I suppose so. And yet—

They stare at each other.

BREEZE: I know what you're thinking, sir. Suppose it isn't Sir Timothy they've seen. Suppose—

HALLAM: Bonaparte has really landed.

BREEZE: That's what you were thinking, wasn't it, sir?

HALLAM: Of course not! Don't be a fool, Sam! From a tunnel! Do you read the newspapers?

BREEZE: Very good, sir.

There is a distant call: Hulloa!

HALLAM: Now, what are we going to do? Have you any suggestions?

BREEZE: Well, sir, it seems to me that the best thing we can do is to get hold of Sir Timothy and keep him quiet until this thing blows over.

HALLAM: I defer to you, Sam. But surely – correct me if I am wrong – surely the point is this: where is Timothy?

BREEZE: That is the point, sir.

Again comes the cry: Hulloa!

HALLAM: I suppose the only thing to do—

BREEZE: Just a minute, sir. Did you hear anything?

HALLAM: No.

BREEZE: I thought I heard—

Again: Hulloa there!

HALLAM: Yes! Yes, indeed.

BREEZE: Oh, what a fool I am!

He goes to the well, and looking down, calls:

Hullo, down there!

He is joined by HALLAM, *they peer into the well.*

TIMOTHY: No, no! Hullo, up here, if you please!

He is above them in the gondola of a gaily painted balloon. He is very happy.

HALLAM: Oh, my God!

TIMOTHY: Fortunes of war! Captured from the enemy with

amazing astuteness. Do I flatter myself? No, I do not.
    HESTER *comes from the house.*

HESTER: Oh, so you're back.

HALLAM: Do you never tread the surface of this earth nowadays, Tim?

TIMOTHY: What an invention! The French have ideas about war. We cannot deny it. Humpage!

HUMPAGE: Sir!

TIMOTHY: May I inform you that in your present position you are completely out of date.

HUMPAGE: Thank you, sir.

TIMOTHY: Hallam, my dear fellow, would you care to come up with me for a while?

HALLAM: Never!

TIMOTHY: You must move with the times. Do you know, I can literally have my head in the clouds.

HESTER: Where did you get it?

TIMOTHY: From the enemy. Found it in a field being guarded by one French soldier. Typical specimen, unshaven and dirty, armed with a form of bill-hook. Didn't appear to understand his own language. I spoke to him – with kindness, you know – and asked him where he came from. *C'est à Bordeaux que vous avez été élevé, je crois, n'est-ce-pas?* I said. The fellow just stared at me, his mouth wide open like an idiot, and then ran away. I suppose he'd never seen an Emperor before. Then I jumped in here, released the anchor, and took to the air. But to national affairs. Hallam, come a little closer. I wish to be secret.
    BREEZE *comes forward.*

BREEZE: Now then, sir, don't you think it would be rather nice if you were to get out of that balloon and come and have a lie down for a while? I'm sure things are going very well at the moment, and so you can take a little time off.

TIMOTHY: You're quite right. Things are going exceedingly

well. But I must not spare myself. I'm needed in the thick of it.

HESTER: Do be careful, Timothy.

BREEZE: I feel you should conserve your energy, sir, for the last great effort.

TIMOTHY: Which is almost upon us, my dear fellow. No, no! I must go on, weary as I am. I could do with a little refreshment. I've had nothing but a few biscuits since breakfast.

BREEZE: Well, you get down from there sir, and I'll go into the house and see what I can find.

TIMOTHY: You do that, but I must remain here ready for instant departure.

HALLAM: It's no good, Sam, no good at all.

TIMOTHY: When I have reported I shall be away again.

HALLAM (*suddenly shouting*): Timothy, get out of that balloon at once!

BREEZE: Now, now, sir, that's not going to help.

HALLAM: I'm sorry, Sam.

TIMOTHY: Tell the family that I am well – desperately tired but well and, as yet, unharmed. I have made contact with the enemy troops twice, and a more slovenly, cowardly, uncouth crew I never did see. I don't know why there's been all this fuss about encountering Bonaparte's much-vaunted army.

BREEZE: Probably, sir, because—

TIMOTHY: Oh, we shan't have any difficulty finishing them off by nightfall. Now then, is there anything else? I don't think so. I brought this report back because I didn't want any of you to worry about me. Tell the others, will you, Hallam. Yes, I think that's all. Stand clear! I am about to ascend!

He begins involved and useless activity about the gondola of the balloon. HESTER *returns to the house.*

HALLAM: Well, Sam?

BREEZE: Well, sir?

HALLAM: This is an unexpected development.

BREEZE: Yes, sir.

HALLAM: There can be no harm in it, I suppose.

BREEZE: Not a bit, sir. The old gentleman will be as safe as houses up there. In a couple of days we can send to fetch him from round about Chichester.

HALLAM: Better than the tunnel, do you think?

BREEZE: Oh, much better, sir. I shouldn't let him go down there again, if I were you.

TIMOTHY: Hallam—

HALLAM: My dear fellow?

TIMOTHY: Can you see anything which might control levitation or propulsion?

HALLAM: Throw something out. Yourself, for example.

   TIMOTHY *jumps up and down in the gondola. This has no effect. There is a bugle call from the beaches.*

TIMOTHY: They're on the move! The French armies! No time to be lost! (*He stares about the balloon in impotent fury.*) Damned useless object! (*Then.*) Humpage!

HUMPAGE: Sir!

TIMOTHY: Pull that thing there and see what happens.

   He points to a ratline from the balloon swinging dangerously near to HUMPAGE's *head.* HUMPAGE *hesitates.*

Well, go on, man – pull it.

   HUMPAGE *does so. The balloon begins to descend.* TIMOTHY, *in sudden realization of this, turns on* HUMPAGE.

You've broken it!

HALLAM (*to* BREEZE): He has, you know.

TIMOTHY: You've let all the – whatever it was filled with – out!

   HUMPAGE *gives another tug at the rope.*

Oh, leave it alone. (*He suddenly understands the exact situation. He is descending the well.*) But I don't want to go down here again!

HUMPAGE: We don't want you to go, sir.

TIMOTHY: Then do something!

Nothing is done. TIMOTHY, *in the gondola of the balloon, descends the well.*

SELINCOURT: Some fool is going round putting out all my signal fires!

HALLAM: That must be so awkward.

SELINCOURT: Awkward! It's disastrous! I'm very, very angry.

HALLAM: Oh, dear!

SELINCOURT: Do you know anything about it?

HALLAM: Nothing – nothing.

SELINCOURT: One man and a little boy ruining everything!

During this the balloon has gently risen from the well, the gondola empty of TIMOTHY, *and begins to float away.* SELINCOURT *notices this.*

What's that?

HALLAM: A balloon.

SELINCOURT: Yours?

HALLAM: No, yours.

SELINCOURT: Ah, yes. Keep an eye on it.

He runs from the garden to return immediately.

I'd better tell you. In a moment we are sealing the entrance to the tunnel.

HALLAM: How?

SELINCOURT: With a ton of explosive. (*He goes out.*)

HALLAM: A ton of explosive! Quickly, Sam!

They move to the well.

Come back to us, Timothy!

BREEZE: Don't alarm him, sir.

HALLAM: I thought, perhaps, a word of encouragement—

BREEZE: Not at the moment. (*He calls down the well.*) Sir Timothy!

HALLAM: Come, Sam, one last great effort.

Together they shout down the well.

BREEZE: I fear it's useless, sir.

In the distance there is a blast on a trumpet. SELINCOURT *shouts:*

SELINCOURT: Stand back! One-two-three-four-five-six.

There is a tremendous reverberating explosion a short way off: also great pandemonium from the FENCIBLES *which fades in the distance.*

HALLAM: Is there anything we can do, Sam?

BREEZE: It doesn't look like it, sir.

But they go off in the direction of the explosion as the MAID-SERVANT *comes from the house.*

MAID: Oh, you're still there, Mr Humpage.

HUMPAGE: Yes, my dear.

MAID: There was a noise, but if you're still there everything must be all right.

HUMPAGE: From the way things are going I shall be up here until the end of time.

MAID: You're the bravest man I know, Mr Humpage.

HUMPAGE: Thank you, my dear.

HESTER *appears in the doorway of the house, and* EDWARD *and* DORCAS *come in from the orchard.*

EDWARD: It's all still here.

DORCAS: Yes. For a little longer. Hold my hand.

HESTER: I thought it was your father.

DORCAS: It may well have been.

HESTER *is regarding a wisp of smoke rising from the well. She looks into the depths.*

HESTER: What's he doing down there now?

DORCAS: You mustn't go down, Mama!

HESTER: Don't be absurd, child. I've no intention of doing so. Your father is quite capable of managing his own affairs. No one seems to understand that. (*She is about to return to the house, when:*) Dorcas—

DORCAS: Mama?

HESTER: You told us earlier – and we were a little sharp with you – that you are in love.

DORCAS: Yes, Mama.

HESTER: I can only presume it to be with this young man.

DORCAS: Yes.

HESTER: What did your father say?

DORCAS: That it was no time to be falling in love. When is a proper time, Mama?

HESTER: Any day of the week. People sometimes smile at the memory of your father and myself, but with us it was a Friday. A perfectly suitable day, like any other. Your father has forgotten, but never mind. What's the time?

DORCAS: Late.

HESTER: Then be happy.

EDWARD: We will. Because I'm going tonight.

DORCAS *pulls herself away from* EDWARD's *hand, and runs from the garden.*

HESTER: For you're not in love.

EDWARD: No.

HESTER: And she knows that. Ah, well, there'll be other summer days for her.

EDWARD *follows* DORCAS.

HESTER *stares after him for a moment, and then speaks to the* MAIDSERVANT.

HESTER: Don't stand gaping, Pippin. Get on with your preparations.

MAID: Yes, ma'am.

As HESTER *and the* MAID *go into the house* HALLAM *and* BREEZE, *escorted by* SELINCOURT *and surrounded by the* FENCIBLES, *return to the garden.*

HALLAM: Listen, sir – I've no wish to be caught further in your machinations.

SELINCOURT: Not mine, Mr Matthews, but the Devil's. Ask Mr Brotherhood.

BROTHERHOOD: True.

SELINCOURT: For we have unearthed him. He is on the run, among us at this very moment. Everyone alert!

HALLAM *and* BREEZE *merely look mystified.*

HALLAM: Mr—

SELINCOURT: Selincourt.

HALLAM (*with grave patience*): Mr Selincourt. Kindly explain yourself. Once again.

SELINCOURT: Certainly. Our explosion – which you heard—

HALLAM: Yes.

SELINCOURT: – was only partially successful.

HALLAM: Continue.

SELINCOURT: Our proposition was, as I told you—

HALLAM: To seal—

SELINCOURT: Correct. To seal the entrance to the tunnel.

HALLAM: Well?

SELINCOURT: And to stifle the beast in the depths. Well, we set the charge—

HALLAM: A ton of explosive.

SELINCOURT: – and formed about the tunnel entrance in a circle.

HALLAM: Admirable!

SELINCOURT: To prevent, you understand, any possible escape.

HALLAM: In the confusion. Yes, go on.

SELINCOURT: All was prepared—

HALLAM: But—

SELINCOURT: – we overlooked one thing.

HALLAM: That being?

SELINCOURT: The size of the charge.

HALLAM: It was—

SELINCOURT: Too great; Piggott, here—

HALLAM: Brave fellow.

SELINCOURT: lit the fuse.

A pause.

HALLAM: Yes?

SELINCOURT: The charge exploded and – here is the error—

HALLAM: Yes?

SELINCOURT: Bonaparte was ejected from the mouth of the tunnel like a bullet from a gun. He flew over our heads—

HALLAM: Amazing sight!

SELINCOURT: – to fall twenty yards beyond the bounds of my cordon.

HALLAM: Unhurt?

SELINCOURT: Apparently. The confusion among my men – understandably – was enormous. And in that confusion Bonaparte made off in this direction. But we shall catch him – never fear – we shall catch him.

LAMPRETT *and the* BOY, *very dirty, come in from the orchard. They are pleased with themselves.*

LAMPRETT: An excellent day's work! Nine conflagrations totally extinguished.

SELINCOURT: You – you!

LAMPRETT: I cannot recall ever having seen you before, sir.

HALLAM (*swiftly*): Mr Selincourt – Mr Lamprett Bellboys.

SELINCOURT: You are the man who has been putting out all my fires.

LAMPRETT: Your fires, sir?

SELINCOURT: Yes.

LAMPRETT: The law holds that a fire, once under way, is public property, sir. Your fires, indeed! But tell me, do you mean you started them?

SELINCOURT: I was responsible.

LAMPRETT: Then you should be ashamed of yourself! A grown man going about the countryside wantonly starting fires.

SELINCOURT: Surely you understand that—

LAMPRETT: If you please, we will discuss the matter no further. They are out.

SELINCOURT: But—

LAMPRETT: Hush! (*He pats the* BOY *on the head.*) Good boy!
>   BREEZE *has now made his way to the orchard gate. Suddenly
>   he cries out:*

BREEZE: Sir!

HALLAM: Yes?

BREEZE (*pointing through the orchard*): There – there!

HALLAM: What?

BREEZE: There he goes!

HALLAM: Sam!

BREEZE: A small man—

SELINCOURT: Yes?

BREEZE: – in a cocked hat—

SELINCOURT: What?

BREEZE: Breeches.

SELINCOURT: My God!

BREEZE: There – there!

SELINCOURT: Bonaparte! (*He joins* BREEZE *at the orchard
gate.*) I can see no one.

BREEZE: Just went down, sir, behind that hedgerow.

SELINCOURT: Fencibles! Follow-follow-follow-follow—
>   *And so shouting he runs out to the orchard,* BROTHERHOOD,
>   GIDDY *and* PIGGOTT *taking after him. There is a pause.*

HALLAM: My dear Sam, what are you doing? Did you see
someone?

BREEZE: No, sir.

HALLAM: I thought not. Then why this extraordinary
exhibition?

BREEZE: You'll know in a moment, sir.
>   *It is a fraction of time and then* BREEZE *points the way from
>   the cliff-top.* TIMOTHY *has appeared. He is very dirty and his
>   clothes are in a most dilapidated state: he retains his hat and the
>   impersonation is yet very recognizable.* HALLAM *goes to him.*

HALLAM: My dear old friend!

TIMOTHY: Hallam!
>   *They embrace.*

Tried to blow me up, the devils. Inefficient fools! Ran
some kind of mine which went off, and up I went like a
rocket. Amazing sensation! Then, while they stood around
gaping, I came to earth. Was rather stunned. Don't quite
know what I did. Have they been here?

HALLAM: Yes. But, Tim, they are not – my word, I am
pleased to see you! – listen, they are not—

BREEZE: Sir!

HALLAM: What is it, Sam?

BREEZE: Ask him if he's seen anyone like himself.

HALLAM: Why?

BREEZE: Well, sir, we just don't know, do we? Whether Sir
Timothy is the one, or whether Boney really is here.

HALLAM: Of course. Listen, Timothy—

TIMOTHY: Um?

HALLAM: This is very important. Have you, in your travels,
seen anyone looking like you?

   There is a pause.

TIMOTHY: You mean someone has been impersonating me?
(*He is suddenly very angry.*) Damned impertinence! Where
is he? Before long I shan't be able to call my life my own.

   LAMPRETT, *who has been standing by regarding all this,*
comments.

LAMPRETT: Well, I'm sure no one else would wish to be
credited with it.

   – *and leaves the garden, taking the* BOY *with him.* BREEZE,
who is still standing by the orchard gate, calls.

BREEZE: Look out, sir!

HALLAM: For what?

BREEZE: They're coming back!

HALLAM: Heavens! They mustn't see him like this. They'll
probably shoot at sight.

BREEZE: They probably will, sir.

HALLAM: In here!

   He begins to bustle TIMOTHY *towards the alcove.*

G

TIMOTHY: My dear Hallam. I'd be very much obliged if you would refrain from jostling me. I'm extremely tired and—

HALLAM: They're here!

TIMOTHY: What's that?

HALLAM *has piloted him into the alcove.*

HALLAM: They're here!

TIMOTHY: Where?

HALLAM: Here!

SELINCOURT, BROTHERHOOD, GIDDY *and* PIGGOTT *march through the garden.* TIMOTHY *speaks to* HALLAM.

TIMOTHY: *Pour la famille, mon cher, pour la famille! (He then steps from the alcove to confront* SELINCOURT *and the* FEN-CIBLES.) *Messieurs! Je suis votre Empereur. Je suis Napoléon Bonaparte. Retirez! Les armées de France sont vaincrent! Retournez à vos domestiques! Allons! Je suis un prisonnier et—*

Then the FENCIBLES, *recovered from their amazement, fall upon him. The confusion is indescribable. At last,* TIMOTHY *stands pinioned by the* FENCIBLES *whilst* SELINCOURT *triumphant, parades before him.*

SELINCOURT: *Aha! Mon petit tyran! Aha! Mon bête sauvage!* (*He tweaks* TIMOTHY's *nose.*)

TIMOTHY: God damn you!

SELINCOURT: Oh, you speak English.

TIMOTHY: *Non.*

SELINCOURT: Well, anyway, we've got you, disgusting little pest.

TIMOTHY: Are you English?

SELINCOURT: Of course I'm English.

TIMOTHY: Then what the hell are you doing? Hallam!

SELINCOURT: Are you Napoleon Bonaparte?

TIMOTHY: *Oui! Non! No!*

SELINCOURT: Of course you deny it. Mr Brotherhood, do you identify this man as the one who stole your biscuits?

BROTHERHOOD: I do.

SELINCOURT: Then, Napoleon Bonaparte, in the King's name I declare you to be my prisoner.

TIMOTHY: Well, if I'm Napoleon Bonaparte who in hell are you?

SELINCOURT: My name is George Selincourt and I am commander of the local forces.

TIMOTHY: Dear God! I'm Bellboys.

SELINCOURT: Who?

TIMOTHY: Timothy Bellboys.

SELINCOURT: So you're Timothy Bellboys, are you? Well, well, well! (*Suddenly very intimidating.*) Impersonation, eh? A knowledge of the local gentry is not going to help you. What have you done with the poor old gentleman—

TIMOTHY: Poor old gentleman!

SELINCOURT: Yes! What have you done with him? Murdered him, probably, and stuffed his frail old body into some hole in the ground. What harm had he ever done to you?

TIMOTHY, *in an excess of fury, attempts to break loose from the* FENCIBLES.

Hold him! Hold him!

TIMOTHY: I tell you I am Timothy Bellboys! Ask my friend, Hallam Matthews, there.

SELINCOURT *turns doubtfully to* HALLAM.

SELINCOURT: Can you identify this man, sir?

HALLAM: Certainly. Lord Nelson.

Then, with BREEZE, *he retires a little way off.*

SELINCOURT (*to* BROTHERHOOD): What do you think?

BROTHERHOOD: It is very difficult to know what to think.

TIMOTHY: Or what to think with, apparently.

SELINCOURT: It will not help to be abusive. We are only trying to determine the truth.

TIMOTHY: And whilst you are determining the truth, the French may be preparing to assault the beaches.

SELINCOURT: That is all taken care of. Mr Brotherhood—

TIMOTHY: Taken care of! You do not impress me, sir.

SELINCOURT: Mr Brotherhood—

> SELINCOURT *and* BROTHERHOOD *confer in whispers.*
>
> TIMOTHY *speaks to* PIGGOTT.

TIMOTHY: Will you have a care! You are pinching my arm quite unmercifully. I think you take a delight in it, you horrid fellow.

> SELINCOURT *and* BROTHERHOOD *have reached a decision.*

SELINCOURT: Now, sir—

TIMOTHY: Well?

SELINCOURT: Are you willing to answer a few questions to prove your identity?

TIMOTHY: No.

SELINCOURT: Then I'm afraid I must insist. Mr Brotherhood here is going to help me.

TIMOTHY: Help you with the questions?

SELINCOURT: Yes.

TIMOTHY: Is anyone going to help me with the answers?

SELINCOURT: Certainly not.

TIMOTHY: Well, unless I'm released you'll get nothing from me.

SELINCOURT (*to* GIDDY *and* PIGGOTT): Release him.

> *They do so, and* TIMOTHY *comes forward.*

Now, sir, at Mr Brotherhood's suggestion I am going to put to you several questions which only an Englishman could answer. Are you ready?

TIMOTHY: Yes.

SELINCOURT: One. What is a Wykehamist?

TIMOTHY: I am a Wykehamist.

> SELINCOURT *looks at* BROTHERHOOD, *who shakes his head.*

BROTHERHOOD: Inconclusive.

TIMOTHY: I can make a guess as to what you are.

SELINCOURT: Two. What was the second question, Mr Brotherhood?

BROTHERHOOD: What is a New Leicester?

TIMOTHY: A cow.

BROTHERHOOD: Oh, very good!

SELINCOURT: Is he right?

BROTHERHOOD: Yes.

TIMOTHY: Aha! Go on.

SELINCOURT: Three. Now this requires action. Watch carefully. If I was to do this – (*With underarm action he bowls an imaginary ball to* TIMOTHY) – what would you do?

TIMOTHY (*very intent*): Do it again.

   SELINCOURT *repeats the action.*

SELINCOURT: Well, what would you do?

TIMOTHY: This!

   With an imaginary bat TIMOTHY *strikes the imaginary ball and then proceeds to run madly between two points some ten yards apart touching down at each imaginary wicket.*

SELINCOURT: Stop! Stop!

   TIMOTHY *stops.*

  Do you play?

TIMOTHY: Cricket? Of course. Do you?

SELINCOURT: Yes, indeed.

TIMOTHY: God bless my soul! What's your name again?

SELINCOURT: Selincourt.

TIMOTHY: Not Stumper Selincourt?

   At this SELINCOURT *positively simpers.*

SELINCOURT: I must confess that I am sometimes known by the appellation – on the field.

TIMOTHY: But you're famous.

SELINCOURT: Oh, come.

TIMOTHY: Yes, you are. And these brave fellows – (*He indicates* BROTHERHOOD, GIDDY *and* PIGGOTT) – are they some of your team?

SELINCOURT: Yes. We have a side, in its infancy yet, but give us a few weeks. I've been working hard with them since my arrival here from Somerset.

TIMOTHY: Then we must play, Stumper Selincourt. Well, well! Hallam, this is Stumper Selincourt.

HESTER *comes from the house. She is dressed in what appears to be a suit of golden armour and is accompanied by the tiny* MAIDSERVANT *who, dressed for travelling, bears the baggage.*

HESTER: Ah! gentlemen—

Everyone seeing HESTER *is momentarily lost in admiration.*

– what is this? A congress of war?

TIMOTHY: We were talking about cricket.

HESTER: At a time like this? I feel you must be joking, Timothy.

HALLAM: The immediate danger would appear to have passed, Hester.

HESTER: Nonsense, Hallam! East Anglia is in turmoil. I set off at once. (*She calls.*) Lamprett!

LAMPRETT *comes in and recognizes his wife.*

LAMPRETT: Oh!

HESTER: Don't be afraid. I'm away now.

They embrace.

LAMPRETT: Goodbye. Come back soon.

TIMOTHY: Breeches or not, Hester, you appear to be amply protected.

HESTER: We can but take care. And if one goes down one should go down magnificently. An Englishman's prerogative.

SELINCOURT *comes to attention as* HESTER *and the* MAID *march out.*

TIMOTHY: I say, are you hungry?

SELINCOURT: A little.

TIMOTHY: I am, damnably. Come inside and we'll find some food. Give us a chance to talk. Now that we've met we must arrange something at once. Come along, all of you.

The FENCIBLES *go into the house.*

I've quite a fair side, although now my sister-in-law has gone it will be weaker, but I think we can give you a game.

In fact, I'm sure we can. (*He takes* SELINCOURT *to the door of the house.*) By the way, this business of my being Bonaparte—

SELINCOURT: Never mind that nonsense!

TIMOTHY: What! (*He roars with laughter.*) Show you my bat. Not bad. Made it myself.

With SELINCOURT *he goes into the house.*

HALLAM: And so, Sam, there is always a basis for understanding, however remote it may appear, however dissimilar the two parties, however hopeless the situation.

BREEZE: Yes, sir.

HALLAM: Comforting, isn't it?

BREEZE: Yes, sir.

HALLAM: And you, Lamprett – a good day?

LAMPRETT: Excellent! I'm just cleaning up the engine – oh, it has done magnificently! – and then I shall go to my bed. It has been a somewhat busy day for you, too, I suppose.

HALLAM: Unwittingly, I have sometimes been caught up in the general action.

BREEZE laughs.

LAMPRETT: Well, you must enjoy the remainder of your stay with us.

HALLAM: Thank you, Lamprett.

LAMPRETT goes out.

BREEZE: Will you come in now, sir?

HALLAM: Not for a while, I think. I propose to revel for a time in this most unaccustomed peace.

BREEZE: Very good, sir. (*He goes into the house.*)

HALLAM: Humpage!

HUMPAGE: Sir!

HALLAM: Anything to report?

HUMPAGE: No, sir.

HALLAM: Thank God.

He wanders a little way off. From within the house comes a subdued burst of men's laughter. Suddenly, the day is gone, it is evening and from the long shadows come EDWARD *and* DORCAS.

DORCAS: What are you going to do in London?

EDWARD: I shall find people who think as I do, and work with them.

DORCAS: Do any women think as you do?

EDWARD: There are some.

DORCAS: Are they beautiful?

EDWARD: Well, it's sad. Nearly all girls with the right ideas – my ideas – seem to have the plainest faces.

DORCAS: I'm glad. I don't think it's sad at all. (*She looks round the garden.*) There hasn't been enough time, Edward. Not enough time to tell each other all that needs to be told.

EDWARD: There never is. When you're properly in love a lifetime isn't long enough.

DORCAS: There has to be a lot of parting in the world.

EDWARD: Yes. Men are cursed with ideas, and ideas aren't much use unless they're put into practice. This means travelling far, going to war, parting from people you love. But there'll come a day, if I have my way, when women will be able to go with men, equally.

DORCAS: Even the beautiful ones?

EDWARD: Even the beautiful ones. Like you. (*Pause.*) I must go now.

DORCAS: Yes. It's all right, I'm not going to cry.

EDWARD: Of course not. Try to believe that what I believe is important.

DORCAS: I do!

EDWARD: People of my kind get laughed at a lot, you know. There is something comic about the very serious. But, all the same, these questions I ask *are* serious. Mr Matthews is the kind of man who laughs to stop himself from crying. That takes a lot of courage. I've never been able to do it.

DORCAS: You mustn't ever do that. You must never change.

EDWARD: I've never cared what people think of me. Somehow I care what you think. (*Pause.*) I must go.

DORCAS: Yes. How will you remember me?

EDWARD: Just as you are.

DORCAS: Neither better nor worse?

EDWARD: No. Just as you are. There are times you remember and times you forget, but your life is made up of the times you remember.

DORCAS: So we shall be a small part of each other's lives, because of today. Kiss me.

EDWARD *does so.*

Goodbye.

LAMPRETT *comes into the garden with the small* BOY. *The* BOY *is dressed as he was on arrival.*

LAMPRETT: I thought you'd be off now. He's all ready.

EDWARD: Thank you.

HALLAM *is approaching.*

LAMPRETT (*to the* BOY): Got everything? Good. I think we did well today. A fine job. Can I give you a word of advice? Out there in the world people will always be telling you not to get caught between two fires. Don't pay any attention to them.

The BOY *is solemn-faced.*

(*to* HALLAM) Why do we always make bad jokes when we part from people we like? What idiots we are.

The BOY *kisses* LAMPRETT.

Oh, that's nice.

HALLAM: Goodbye, Mr Sterne, and good luck. I don't know what you're going to do when you get to London, but with your ideas you should start a theatre.

LAMPRETT: You see! We all do it.

HALLAM: I'm sorry.

DORCAS *is buttoning the* BOY's *coat. She speaks to him.*

DORCAS: *Adieu, mon petit pompier. Bon voyage. Tu vas. Tu as de la chance, toi. Je reste. Adieu.*

EDWARD *and the* BOY *go.*

LAMPRETT: What did you say, Dorcas?

DORCAS: I said goodbye. He's French.

HALLAM: A little enemy!

LAMPRETT: French! God bless my soul! I'd never have known it. There are children in the village who look just like that.

DORCAS: It will teach you a lesson. Both of you. Never treat children in a childish way. That boy has stood on battle-fields, he's walked continents, he's been threatened and survived, he's seen the dead, he's swum rivers and gone hungry. My God, he makes you look innocent. He makes you look – like children.

    DORCAS *moves away to a point where she can stand looking over the countryside.* TIMOTHY *comes from the house. He has changed from his uniform of impersonation and now wears a dressing robe. He carries a cricket bat.*

TIMOTHY: I say, Hallam, this Selincourt is an amazing fellow. Tells me he once stumped Richard Nyren. You know, the captain of Hambledon.

HALLAM: Really!

TIMOTHY: Yes, he did. And he's as modest as milk about it. By the way we're arranging a match for next Sunday. Think you'll be here then?

HALLAM: I doubt that, Tim.

TIMOTHY: Pity. Now that Hester's gone I've got to find another player and – (*He holds up his bat.*) – I thought you might care to—

HALLAM: No.

TIMOTHY: I could teach you in an afternoon.

HALLAM: No, Timothy.

TIMOTHY: Then Humpage will have to come down.

HUMPAGE: Can I believe my ears?

LAMPRETT: No, you cannot, Humpage. Whatever can you be thinking of, Timothy? Humpage has his duties.

TIMOTHY: Yes, I suppose so.

    HUMPAGE *groans.*

Well, Lamprett, I'll have to show you, I suppose. (*He gives the bat to* LAMPRETT.) Try not to make too big a fool of yourself. Oh, God! You're holding it by the wrong end, man.

LAMPRETT: Well, I can't see.

TIMOTHY: Come inside and I'll show you. I hope you're enjoying your stay with us, Hallam.

HALLAM: I am, very much – at the moment.

TIMOTHY: Don't seem to have had a chance to say it before, but I'll say it now. We're very pleased to see you, Hallam. Aren't we, Lamprett?

LAMPRETT: Of course.

TIMOTHY: There's some food and drink inside when you're ready for it.

HALLAM: Bless you, Tim.

TIMOTHY: You're happy, then?

HALLAM: Very happy, thank you.

TIMOTHY: Good. Now, Lamprett, as a beginner you'll have to go in the outfield.

LAMPRETT: Where's that?

TIMOTHY: You'll find out.

LAMPRETT: Is it a dangerous game?

TIMOTHY: Well, you want to look out for your knuckles, you know—

Together TIMOTHY *and* LAMPRETT *go into the house. The garden becomes darker. A great branched candlestick, ablaze, is placed in the window of a ground floor room of the house. From within the house comes a second burst of laughter and, for a moment, a single voice is raised in a snatch of song. Distantly, from the beaches, a bugle sounds the Stand Down.* DORCAS *can be seen against the night sky looking out over the countryside. After a moment she enters the garden to move to* HALLAM *and sit beside him. They remain together in silence for a considerable time. At last* HALLAM *speaks to her.*

HALLAM: Not tears to end the day.

When DORCAS *speaks her voice is high and clear.*

DORCAS: I'm not crying. Didn't you know, Mr Matthews, that you do not cry over spilt milk or lost lovers.

HALLAM: I'm sorry.

DORCAS: It's quite all right. (*There is a pause.*) You don't mind if I sit here with you for a while?

HALLAM: Not at all, darling.

DORCAS: Please don't be kind to me.

HALLAM: I'm sorry.

DORCAS: And please don't continue to be sorry. You have given no offence. I shall sit here for a while because I don't know where to go. I've not yet made up my mind, you understand?

In the slight pause, the sudden rush of an evening breeze seems to disturb the stillness of the garden.

Can you see me?

HALLAM: Yes.

DORCAS: It is getting dark. Day's end. Nightfall. I suppose there will be a tomorrow. (*A pause.*) I cannot believe that I shall wake to find the sun high. (*A pause.*) Do you know a song beginning 'All my past life is mine no more—'?

HALLAM: 'All my past life is mine no more;
     The flying hours are gone,
     Like transitory dreams given o'er,
     Whose images are kept in store
         By memory alone.'

Yes, I know that.

DORCAS: I wondered if you did. There is no need to talk if you do not wish.

BREEZE *comes from the house.*

BREEZE: Mr Matthews—

HALLAM: I'm here, Sam.

BREEZE: That's everything then, sir.

HALLAM: Thank you, Sam.

BREEZE: Thank you, sir. Goodnight, Miss Bellboys.

DORCAS: Goodnight.
BREEZE: Goodnight, sir.
HALLAM: Goodnight, Sam. God rest you.

BREEZE *goes out by the orchard. It is now almost dark but for the light of the night sky and the blaze of the candles in the window. From within the house a spinet strikes up a tune and men's voices, gay and gentle, begin to sing.* HUMPAGE *stirs in his sleep and the brass bell sounds once, softly. The tune ends. A single star stands in the sky.*

CURTAIN

NOTES

The Title is explained by the quotation from Yeats on page xvii. In Germany the play was given a new title which could be translated as *When We Were Happy*, and John Whiting thought it a good one.

Page 1 (Stage directions). *1804:* At this date England had resumed the long war with France that began in 1792 and was interrupted by the short-lived Peace of Amiens (1802). Now Napoleon had assembled a fleet at Boulogne and the imminent invasion was the subject of much apprehension and rumour, especially on the Dorset coast.

p. 2. *alfresco:* in the open air (Italian).

p. 5. *an exquisite, a dandy:* both words describe a man who is excessively elegant in his clothes or refined in his manner.

p. 7. *William Wordsworth* (1770–1850): had upset conservative people by his revolutionary ideas about both poetry and politics. He had originally welcomed the French Revolution ('Bliss was it in that dawn to be alive', he wrote), but he later became troubled by the way in which its principles were betrayed, especially by Napoleon. By his determination to read Wordsworth, Hallam shows that he wants to keep up with the latest developments in poetry and that his mind is not closed to political ideas different from his own.

p. 10. *Humpage crosses himself:* This is his reaction to Timothy's prophecy of coming trouble. He makes the sign of the cross to ward off evil spirits or influences.

p. 11. *mercenary:* Men like Sir Timothy think of war as a noble and romantic activity in which patriots fight for their country and heroes for their principles. Edward Sterne's experience is of armies full of soldiers fighting merely as a means of earning a poor living.

p. 11. *subscribed:* here means *submitted to the authorities.*

p. 14. *'Linden:* Hohenlinden (already mentioned). A French victory over Austria in 1800, which prepared the way for the Peace of Amiens. This Peace, which included England, was greeted with rejoicing throughout a Europe wearied by nine years of war, but it lasted only fourteen months. The resumption of fighting is usually blamed on Napoleon's ambition to dominate Europe.

p. 20. *mantraps:* steel spring traps set on private land to catch (and often maim) trespassers. They were eventually made illegal because they were so inhuman.

p. 22. *Horace Walpole* (1717–97): son of the statesman Sir Robert

Walpole. Distinguished author and leader of literary and artistic taste. Famous as a letter-writer.

p. 25. *Tintinnabulum pueri:* an attempt to render Bellboys into Latin.

p. 26. *jawbone of an ass:* This is a joking reference to the story told in the Bible (*Judges* 15) of how Samson killed numbers of his enemies with a jawbone of an ass as weapon.

p. 30. *The Rights of Man:* (1791) the principal work of Thomas Paine. Paine was born in Norfolk in 1737; went to America in 1774, fought and wrote for the American colonists in the War of Independence and was influential in framing the Declaration of Independence (1776). In 1787 he returned to England. *The Rights of Man* was written in answer to Burke's attack on the French Revolution. It provoked great anger, and in 1792 Paine was indicted for treason and escaped to France, where he was welcomed and made a member of the Convention. Meanwhile his ideas and writings were rigorously suppressed, and Edward Sterne in the play needs courage to quote *The Rights of Man*. Paine died in poverty in America in 1809.

p. 31. *Jeremy Bentham* (1748–1832): philosopher and legal reformer, who asserted that the purpose of law-making should be to provide the greatest happiness for the greatest number.

Page 31. *Jean-Jacques Rousseau* (1712–78): philosopher whose ideas prepared the way for the French Revolution. He blamed society for the ills of mankind, and thought that men brought up in absolute freedom would be naturally good.

p. 32. *tricolour:* The red, white and blue flag of France adopted after the Revolution.

p. 33. *Boodles:* a very exclusive London club.

p. 34. *fuzee:* a kind of match applied to a cannon to ignite the explosive.

Page 34. *linstock:* a staff with a fork at one end to hold the fuzee.

p. 36. *Beast of the Apocalypse:* The Apocalypse is the last book in the New Testament, usually called *Revelation*. It contains a prophecy of Armageddon, where disaster overwhelms Mankind, when the 'bottomless pit' of Hell will be opened and 'the beast that is to ascend from the bottomless pit' will make war upon them. Here Napoleon is thought of as the fiend in the prophecy. He is also the Serpent (Satan) of Corsica, where he was born.

p. 45. *baton:* a joking illusion to the saying attributed to Napoleon that every French soldier carried in his haversack the baton of a Marshal of France (i.e. could rise to the highest rank).

p. 46. *Lord Nelson* (1758–1805): was to Englishmen the popular hero as Napoleon was the hated enemy. He was killed in the hour of his greatest victory, in the sea-battle of Trafalgar.

p. 49. *Armageddon* is the place where in *Revelation* (ch. 16) the kings of the world are assembled for war – 'and a great earthquake such as had never been since men were on the earth'.

p. 51. '*Drink not the third glass* . . .': a quotation from *The Temple*, by George Herbert (1593–1633), a religious poet referred to later.

p. 52. *merrythought:* a wishbone, the forked bone in front of a fowl's breastbone.

p. 59. *the head of the state:* George III (1738–1820) suffered throughout his reign from fits of mental derangement and became permanently insane in 1811.

p. 59. *who's just had himself crowned:* Napoleon, denying the democratic principles by which he had risen to power, had himself proclaimed Emperor of the French. The Pope came to Paris to consecrate him, but Napoleon actually placed the crown on his own head. (This happened in December 1804 – i.e. *after* the date given by the author to the events of the play.)

p. 59. *Napoleon's family:* Napoleon made his brother Joseph King of Naples and later Spain, Jerome King of Westphalia, and Louis King of Holland. (But all these appointments were actually made after the events of this play.)

p. 60. *de la Rochefoucauld:* (1613–1680). French writer, soldier and courtier. The quotation is from *Maximes*, a collection of epigrammatic and cynical observations on life and society.

p. 63. *alfresco:* See note on p. 90.

p. 63. *George Herbert:* Poet already quoted by Hallam. That food was wrapped in a page of his poems suggests a decline in his reputation. The detail indicates Brotherhood's meticulous reporting.

p. 63. *exorcism:* expelling of evil spirits by prayers or ceremonies.

p. 78. Neither Sir Timothy's nor Selincourt's Erench should be taken as a model!

p. 80. *Wykehamist.* Person educated at Winchester College, founded 1584 by William of Wykeham.